MW00472579

BERBER ODES

Poetry from the Mountains of Morocco

A Collection of the Poetry of Place

Edited by

MICHAEL PEYRON

ELAND • LONDON

This arrangement and commentary © Michael Peyron 2010

ISBN 978 1 906011 28 4

First published in November 2010 by Eland Publishing Ltd,
61 Exmouth Market, Clerkenwell, London EC1R 4QL

Pages designed and typeset by Antony Gray
Cover image: L'Oued de Bou Saada
by Eugène Alexis Girardet
Printed and bound in Spain by
GraphyCems, Navarra

Contents

INTRODUCTION

The poems in this volume come for the most part from the Middle Atlas (formerly Fazaz) region in north-central Morocco, a land of rugged mountains, oak and cedar forests, unlikely lakes and gushing torrents. They are representative of a particularly rich, Heroic Age culture that has survived in oral form, more or less unimpaired, down to the present day among the pastoral, Tamazight-speaking pastoral communities of the area. Some, belonging to the repertoire of village bards, consist of two-, three-, or four-line pieces of an amorous, amusing or pedagogical nature, featuring alliteration and assonance, not to mention a turn of phrase not usually found in everyday speech. These pieces contain certain cultural allusions and hidden meanings, understandable only to a local audience. Comparatively easy to memorize, they circulate over hill and dale, becoming common property to an entire segment of Morocco's rural population. They will be sung by shepherds on some barren hillside, by grass-cutting maidens in the fields; many will give rise to song and dance, in connection with the famous Middle Atlas *ahidus* tradition.

Other more elaborate poems refer to historical events. Between 30 and 100 lines long, they are somewhat reminiscent of the lyrical ballads of Britain's Romantic period, though varied in content (elegiac, pedagogical, religious, historical, prophetic, political, etc.). These are works of art in their own right, stemming from the repertoire of some wandering bard (*amdyaz*), featuring a combination of 'gift of the gab', inspiration and recourse to well-tried formulae, which can only be produced by practitioners who have mastered their craft. Indeed, memorisation and recitation tax the poet's skills to the limit, while a highly critical audience will be just as quick to censure shortcomings as to praise a polished performance. It takes a professional troubadour – the likes of Moha ou Lyazid, or today's Sheikh Zayd Lisiwr – to guarantee praise.

Contrary to classic verse of the European or Arabian kind, Berber poetry very rarely features end-rhyme. It does, however, contain phonetic parallelism of some kind, usually in the shape of internal rhyme, alliteration and assonance. In all poems belonging to the Heroic Age period, that is up to 1932, the translator has used old-fashioned forms: thee, thy, thine, canst, didst, etc.; for more recent pieces, however, except in cases where the poet addresses himself directly to God, such archaisms have been abandoned.

For nearly twenty years I have been working on the various Middle Atlas poetic genres, recording items in the field, or accessing material in the Berber archives at Aix-en-Provence. This collection runs the full gamut from humorous, pithy, contemporary couplets to lengthy historical ballads of yesterday retracing the momentous events of the early twentieth century. It focusses on the French military invasion that marked the end of the Heroic Age for Morocco's Imazighen – to give the Berbers their true name.

Other Berber-speaking areas in Morocco, namely the Rif and Sous, have not been totally neglected. The Rif area, a rugged chunk of land dominating the Mediterranean, is home to a hardy breed of mountain peasants, known for their past expertise in war and vendetta. These Tarifit-speakers were in particular close and hostile contact with their Spanish neighbour, who proved to be their chief enemy in the early twentieth century. Some poetry from this tragic period is contained hereunder, together with material of a lighter nature.

Last, but not least, we devote a sizeable section to an area that arguably contains the richest fund of poetry in Morocco: the Tashelhit-speaking Berber south-west region, embracing the

Marrakech High Atlas, Sous plain and Anti-Atlas. A zone of transition between the Sahara and the Atlantic Plain, alternating between date-palmed oases and snow-capped mountain ranges, it is a tough, semi-arid land that has bred a dour type of peasant, industrious and with a bent for commercial transaction – the famous Shelluh grocers, open almost round the clock, that one finds from Agadir to Neuilly. Thanks to the endeavours of an early twentieth-century French officer named Léopold Justinard, a pioneer in this field and better known as *qebtan shluh*, we have access to their poetic tradition. It features an extensive corpus devoted to the region's troubled past, a Heroic Age based on notions of bravery and honour, similar in all respects to those found in the Middle Atlas, with famous *igurramn* (saints) like Sidi Hmad u-Musa, and heroines and heroes like Yamina Mansur and Yahya Umghar. Oft-repeated symbols such as the falcon, the gazelle or the mouflon epitomize courage and tenacity, as much in battle as in the chase. This Shelluh culture boasts a veritable genius for oral literature, specifically the ability to indulge in *amarg*-style love poetry, a genre that features in the repertoire of each *rayss*, whether bards of yesteryear like Si Hemmu Taleb and El-Hajj Belaïd, or their contemporary counterparts, such as Mohamed Demsiri, Hmad Amentag, Omar Ahrouch, Akhattab; or *rayssa*, as lady singers are called: Rqiya Damsiria, Fatima Tabaamrant, or Tihihit Tamezziant.

Whichever area they come from their poems reflect the preoccupations of a Muslim society, in which the emphasis is placed on belief in the Almighty, trustworthiness, group solidarity, defence of the homeland, honour, hospitality and valour.

MICHAEL PEYRON

Visiting Professor History and Culture of the Berbers, Al-Akhawayn University, Ifrane (Morocco)

GLOSSARY

agurram, pl. *igurrman*	saint, marabout
ahellel	a form of religious chant
ahidus	traditional Middle Atlas Berber dance
ahwawi	dissolute youngster
amarg	poetry, love, melancholy
amazan	envoy, go-between
amdyaz, pl. *imdyazn*	troubadour, wandering musician
barud	gun-powder
burtgiz	Portuguese
Fazaz region	historical, pre-twentieth century name of Middle Atlas
hakem	resident French administrative officer
harka	military expedition
hurm	sacred sanctuary
képi [Fr.]	French officer's pill-box cap
biru (*bureau* [Fr.])	administrative outpost
qaçida	epic, or religious poem
qayd	local notable (usually spelled caïd)
rayss, fem. *rayssa*	band-leader
rrami, pl. *rrma*	sharpshooter
tayffart	chain of couplets, forming verse ballad
tamawayt, pl. *timawayin*	poetic strophe sung in a high-pitched voice
tamdyazt	verse ballad
ttalb, pl. *ttelba*	preacher
uday, pl. *udayn*	Jew, coward, non-arms-bearing person

CLASSIC ORAL POETRY FROM THE MIDDLE ATLAS

Battle of Baht

Woman! Tarry a while, leave not; tell us truthful tidings!
Berbers beguil'd and benighted, their expectations thwarted,
May they ne'er again from sweet spring quench their thirst!
Abhorrent the wayward nation that forsook the path of Islam!
'Abu Ghufayr is our Prophet!', such was their proud boast.
Eternal shame on the unworthy mother of such liars!
Didst thou not hear, didst thou not see, on Baht's battle-field?
Didst thou not hear groans rising behind the war-steeds' hooves?
Moans and wails of mothers tearful, their babes trampl'd; others
Uttering screams of terror, losing the very milk from their breasts.
On Judgment Day shall the men of Tamesna know that Yunes will
    be riding there with his father's sons, leading on the Berbers
    ever faithful to his cause.
'May Hell's Gates crush him and his line! See there Waryawara,
Chief of the proud ones! This day shall ye triumph not, though
Triumph ye shall in the night of ignorance; 'twas yet the case when
    for Maysara you did fight!'

This is probably the oldest surviving poetic piece containing reference to Berbers. A tenth-century epic fragment, it was allegedly written by Saïd Ibn Hisham al-Masmudi, himself a Berber yet an orthodox Muslim and thus highly critical of the Barghawata. Waryawara ('the incomparable one'), or Yunes, was leader of the

Barghawata heretics who, after Maysara's anti-Arab rebellion, set up an independent princedom – complete with Koran in Berber – in the Tamesna province on Morocco's Atlantic Plain from the 8th to the 12th centuries. The battle of Baht was one of the most savage episodes in the many wars the Barghawata undertook to force neighbouring tribes to bow down to their rule.

The blacksmith's hammer ringeth

Upon the anvil the blacksmith's hammer ringeth!
The bottomless tarn hath yielded dead men's bones,
Ichou Arrok's mighty cedars by lightning blasted,
Ominous signs were seen, mountain clans mustering.
Gathering in arms at Ich Taalam, in Marmoucha hills,
Forsake not thy pastures, O Ayt Idrasen, brave men all,
The warriors of Jbel Fazaz have heeded the call.
Men of Amghas and Tizunin, repair hotfoot to Tafrant Ij,
The Imzinaten of Tumlilin, allies of the Imhiwash saints,
Have with the men of Tabaynut joined hands!
Assemble post-haste at Siqsus and Tafudayt!
In every village, one can hear the hammering!
Fleet-footed messengers race east and west.
Before their sheikh the Imazighen did declare:
'Upon the anvil the blacksmith's hammer ringeth!
From Maghrib thou didst vow to banish the alien kind.
Their lands thou promis'd us, their women, their kine!
Now lead on that we may march forth against the foe!
Upon the anvil the blacksmith's hammer ringeth!'

A traditional verse, author unknown, probably a fragment from a much longer oral ballad, now lost. Translated from the French; cf. M. Le Glay (1922, 82–4).

The action in this poem dates back to the early nineteenth century when, under their saintly leader Bu Bker Amhawsh, the Middle Atlas Imazighen were defying the sultan's army, and all those 'who spoke Arabic in Morocco.'

Ballad of the slain hunter

O Ali Wulluben, O father, wherefore hast committed felony so foul?
O father, remember, wast honour-bound the slain hunter to protect.
Thy daughter asketh thee, O Ali Wulluben, where hath my hunter
    gone?
Felt he aggriev'd? 'Tis perhaps the reason he went without leave-
    taking.
Here's the game-bag he left in our tent – 'twas but a paltry
    parting!
One of the hunters he met probably invited him into his tent.
May God lay waste thy lands, O Ayt Wahi!
May he send swordsmen to slay thee, O Ali Wulluben!
May God inflict backache on Hammu of Ayt Wahi,
Barren make his fields and deprive him of progeny!
Ba w-Musa a-hunting he did go, headed for Lmenakher,
Saw where the eagle was smitten, O vultures vile, the hero's blood
    did find!
Did visit the place where the hunter was set upon, some tracks did
    see.
He follow'd them to where the grass was stain'd with the brave
    man's blood!
O huntsmen, the hero perish'd in a remote spot, dastardly deed
    un-witness'd!
I have yet to wear mourning garb for my huntsman, to scratch my
    cheeks!

His white steed they did sell, the money handed to the man
      Lbessir, saying:
'Thou art a stranger from Zayan, whom nobody will suspect!
If folk notice we have this money, with murder they'll charge us!'
O musketeers, who with dogs do hunt o'er hill and dale,
Will ye not arise, smite the murderer and avenge thy brother?!
Thy crime, O blackguard, hath offended autumn, that drier-up of
      streams,
To God and his Prophet we do appeal! When e'er thou seest wind-
      whipp'd
Tree, O murderer, 'twill be from Muha Lahssen Laaydi – a reminder!

This unpublished poem was recited to me in the spring of 1993 by Fatima
Elasri, Hajj Qeddur, whose parents originally came from the Ayn Luh region.
Interestingly, around 1930, Muha w-Driss (one of Arsène Roux's informants)
had collected an almost identical poem, also in the Ayn Luh region, which
speaks volumes as to the efficiency of oral transmission.

The ballad relates the murder of Muha Lahssen Laaydi, a member
of a hunting confraternity, by one of his fellow hunters, a certain
Hammu of Ayt Wahi, aided and abetted by Ali Wulluben, the
victim's very own father-in-law. Ba w-Musa is another hunter who
finds evidence of the crime in the forest. Normally members of
these *rrma* ('marksmen') communities were under oath of total
solidarity towards each other, which makes the deed even more
heinous. The action belongs to the pre-Protectorate period, which I
have described elsewhere as the Heroic Age of the Atlas Berbers.

Ballad of the old hunter

Pray to the Prophet who surpasseth me, tho' none
Doth surpass the Almighty, who reigneth over all!
Supreme is his power; may my offerings reach him!
Accept my greetings, ignore them not;
To all hunters we do grant mutual forgiveness!
Like reeds are my enfeebl'd knees, devoid of marrow.
Go in peace; however, inform thee I must, O forested peaks!
As strength faileth my shots go wide of the mark.
The lion leader met his black-maned colleague, to him did say:
'I do swear, by the wayside can sleep in the midday heat;
Dagger and musket-ball can harm us no more!
Gone the hunters; as for the musketeers none remain!'
What a fine gazelle in full apparel, seen up at the pass;
Like a woman in belted caftan did tease the hunter, as
She glided slowly past.
Thus spake the boar: 'Let me be, thou who dost pursue me;
Why hunt me so?
'Tis sinful to eat my meat, my hide no useful purpose serveth.'
'Lord, if I miss that beast, may my legs their strength regain!
O tusk'd miscreant, how can thou be bliss incarnate?!'
'Death to thee, O jackal, thou art the one who grindeth gun-powder,
Thou cowardly sheep-stealer!
Doth frighten the children each time he attacketh the herd.'
My faithful gun and constant companion, O Athman of mine,
Will ne'er fail me in places fraught with danger!
Inquire of our fellow-hunters which gun they prefer; all do
Answer: 'Aasila!'
Discard the Ddriha musket; 'tis like the unworthy wife whose
Word you cannot trust!
Her lesson will ne'er learn, 'cause of her stubborn pride!

Respecting the huntsmen's code is like the dutiful housewife
Who carefully churneth her butter-milk.
In her bucket of butter one speck of dirt ne'er shalt find.
Let's ask the white-cloaked hunters which weapons they use;
Regarding the Tasedda musket their replies are unflattering:
'Finely decorated is this gun, but 'tis a costly one; its bullets
Go wide of the mark!
The hunter's hand it woundeth; 'tis not to be relied upon!'
Pray to the Prophet; I follow the straight and narrow path,
O Lord, allow me to cross the river!
Have lost my footing in the swift-flowing current; will be
By the torrent swept away!
Pray to the Prophet! Thou hast fail'd me, O Earth; therein lieth
No salvation!

Here below am an outcast; succour can come but from above!
Pray to the Prophet, he who doth stand by my side;
How can one tire of the Chosen One?
Neither harsh nor tedious be his words to the ear,
Invoke the Prophet, thou the spur on which resteth the foot,
O saddle wherein the Koran is seated!
O Father of all prosperity, take up the staff of all Muslims!

Previously unpublished, and garnered from Fatima Elasri (1993). The Roux
archive also features a similar poem, collected in the 1930s.

This is another example of a traditional oral ballad of the *ahellel* kind,
common to the Ayt Myill of the Ayn Luh area. Typical of semi-
religious Berber verse, it contains several sections: firstly, a preamble
dedicated to God, secondly, a complaint by an old hunter who can
no longer shoot straight, thirdly, a discussion concerning the merits
of different guns, and finally, a panegyric addressed to God and the
Prophet.

Ballad of the valiant shepherd

Thy name first I utter, O Lord, good companion of
Those who do mount their steeds en route for Mecca.
Overcome by heat, to secluded spring my weary feet
Now drag me, my thirst for to quench.
'Tis Ayesha I find there, who, in the company of
Other women, is filling her pitcher at the spring.
'O Ayesha, in God's name, give me a drink of water,
My hand hath been by musket-ball shatter'd.
How can I scoop up water? My wound paineth me
Greatly, cannot be to water expos'd!'

'Thy servant am I not!' answereth she, 'have
Overmuch work to do, my duties cannot neglect!
Rebuked shall I be if I give thee a drink, 'tis what I
Fear most! O ragamuffin, now get thee hence!'
She had yet to finish filling her pitcher. Imagine my
Delight when, lo and behold, her veil came loose!
As she turn'd round, some water did spill; thinking
Better of it, she invited the man in rags to sit and talk.
A shepherd came running, did call out: 'O Ayesha,
The enemy hath raided us, made off with our goats!'

Thus did she speak: 'Well, my friend, do thy duty!
Of the fine musket on thy shoulder make good use!
Bring back my herd to a safe spot', she implor'd,
'On this my day of misfortune do me a good deed!'
'O Ayesha!' the coward replied, 'How in God's
Name can I contrive to bring back your herd?
Have naught but my knapsack. Now, were I to
Have a friend to bring me a full powder pouch!'

Quoth the shepherdess, 'What have we come to!
Didst thou ever see such unmanly behaviour?!
Consider that honest young lad, my chosen one,
Whom fear hath so easily vanquish'd!'

Now, reader, who is to save that dark-eyed beauty,
Is ready to lay down his life, is about to heed her call?
Up riseth the ragamuffin, the goats followeth forthwith,
Skilfully doth return with the herd to the encampment.
Then did the ragged one speak: 'In God's name,
Good people, may ye extend to me welcome most warm!
As for thee, young lady, take back those unworthy
Words you utter'd: 'O ragamuffin, now get thee hence!''
Thus did the girl answer: 'In God's name I do declare,
When death claims thee, shalt be honour'd with tombstone
White, thy grave for to mark, O lion of the deep thickets,
From craven cowards who flee to distinguish thee!'

This traditional ballad of the *tayffart n-tefsutt* genre was recited
to Arsène Roux by Sheikh Hmad u-Ali, a troubadour from the
Ayt Sliman clan, Ayt Yahya of the Tunfit region; I translated the
original text from Berber (Ifrane, 2000) with help from Labha
Elasri and Ayesha Azzawi.

Though the action takes place in the pre-Protectorate period, the
text was originally collected around 1914–18 at Lhajeb. The
narrator uses a device characteristic of Berber poetry-pronominal
ambiguity – when he switches from the first person to the third
person in the fourth stanza. Thus does the ragamuffin hero deliver
the goods; a vivid reminder that in a traditional society based on
very strong notions of manliness and honour, *l'habit ne fait pas le
moine* ('do not judge an individual by the cut of his jib') a young
man convicted of cowardice can easily become a kind of non-
person, as in the following poem.

The coward's tale

O Deity eternal, whose name I first pronounce, keep me
From the Hereafter, e'en though I suffer not Here Below.
May I know happiness, O thou who in the mill dost live,
With abundant waters shalt grind grain divine!
O Deity eternal, whose name I first pronounce, keep
Far my plough from the rock 'neath furrow hidden!
O Deity eternal, whose name I first pronounce, inspire my
Muse, give her thread aplenty that I may spin my yarn!
A skilful swordsman is locked in argument with the
Generous man; to him doth say: 'Stronger am I than thee!'
The table is prepar'd, the meal can begin, yet the two
Diners start quarrelling, disagree over food distribution!

Whereupon the alarm soundeth: 'To arms, villagers, raiders
Have with our flocks made off!' Like a hero Lghazi riseth,
Sword in hand; saddling his steed, spake thus:
'Weep not, O women! This day I die, else I shall return!'
Likewise, the coward his trigger-less musket took, saying:
''Fore God! Shall this day smite them hip and thigh!'
Only to flee, on seeing the dust and smoke of battle:
'Fight well, comrades!' quoth he, 'Must return home,
Fetch weapon fit for fighting! 'Twas the wrong one I took!'
Unworthy man, hard times are these, yet did I not see thee
Hiding straw, instead of sharing with thy neighbours!

Woe betide thee, whereas we live by bandits surrounded,
On the day of battle, your musket is unfit for use!
Unsatisfactory be this young man's comportment –
A good-for-nothing, ill-matched to our community!
Have watch'd the *uday* disport himself at weddings;
The drum doth take, singeth odes to pretty maidens!

Like a great troubadour doth behave, a would-be lion,
Danceth a debased parody of the traditional *ahidus*!
Shame on those fearful, fallen beings, mere exhibitionists!
Shame on maidens who with these individuals consort!
Shame on their milk-white breasts, their exquisite tattoos,
Sullied by the fingers of the lasciviously inclined coward!

Another traditional ballad of the *tayffart n-tefsut* genre, attributed
to Sheikh Seyd, flute-player to the great Sheikh Muhand Aajmi. The
poem was originally recited to Arsène Roux by Assu u-Seyd in
Meknes, 1923. It was translated in Ifrane by me in the spring of
2001 with help from Ayesha Azzawi and Labha Elasri.

The subject matter is very similar to that of the previous poem,
highlighting the emphasis placed on unflinching bravery in the
Berber Heroic Age social code. The term *uday* may be glossed as
'Jew', but also means a coward or non-arms-bearing individual.

Beauty is like unto the rat

O Lord! Sanctified be thy name, thou that dost escort
Pilgrims, 'tis after poetry that my heart pineth!
I sing of a jealous husband, who neither slumber nor
Decency knoweth; jealousy, art like malady unto him!
Art like unto the laggard male lamb, sloth of step.
To his friend the messenger did go and from him
Received directions to his lover's tent, also took
Some garments, sufficient his nakedness for to hide.
The go-between clothed himself, grasped his stout staff,
As if towards Mecca were following the pilgrims' way.
Arrived in an encampment to him recommended,
The tent-pegs did seize, to be taken in as a guest.

Quoth he: 'Hospitality 'fore God! O noble folk!
O mistress of the tent, to me was thy name mention'd!'
The jealous husband, as was his wont, thus did reply:
'Fadma, grant a handful of grain to this vagabond,
'Tis enow; then send him about his business!'
Thus spake she: 'Come close, O beggar, thy blessing on us,
Sooth to say, with my husband am honour bound to stay!'
Quoth he: 'Look you, even though of money be bereft,
As a messenger to thee I come this day! Thy lover asketh:
'Whither be our tryst? To these straits am I reduced! ''
Quoth she: 'Travel on thy way till a certain Thursday,
A dove thou shalt find; go then to water-filled cavern,
Upon seeing my jealous husband do thou take a stone,
Then from bondage shall the dove be releas'd!'

For upwards of a week the vagabond did roam,
Dreaming of the dove that he would find!
'Am not simple-minded, nor have my garments lost,
Beloved, 'twas passion that sent me on my travels!'
Went on his way and the fifth day a dove did descry;
Headed forthwith for the cavern where water floweth.
The damsel his garments to water did commit:
'Wash these, poor wretch, that I may cleanse thee!'
The jealous husband a stone did take, releasing the dove;
She and the wretch abandon'd themselves to love.
As she lay by his side to her did say: 'O Fadma!
Beautiful is thy face. Speak: art with me to stay?'

Answer'd she: 'Strong is the sun, my face with henna
Besmirch'd, in this manner I can other folk no longer see!'
Quoth he: 'Beware, O Fadma, on saint's tomb, oath of
Fidelity we swore; beware now, betray me not!'
By his side she walk'd a few steps, saying,

'In vain thou prayest! Marry, by the saint's name,
I do declare, few folk are here to indulge in prayer!'
Consider now this perjurious, pact-breaking female!
But canst thou, reader, women's wiles resist?
Of beauty am afeard, as with lake-cleansing streams,
More potentially hazardous than the deepest well!

Beauty is like unto a jeweller; should he fine wares
Fashion, doth ask the copper-smith to do it for him!
Beauty is like unto a rat with forty bolt-holes; e'en
If thou shouldst block one, escapeth through the other!
O wicked woman, whither shalt thou solace seek?
Tempt not the hedgehog, thy match shalt surely meet!
Of hidden breasts shalt not obtain the least peep,
Unless a coin is spent; everything cometh at a price!
Westerly winds can saplings goad to frenzy;
As for venerable tree-trunks, they remain unbending!
Now, what's to be done? With the barber or with
Shepherds brawl? Would that my neighbours spare me!
O Mulay Muhand, to thee my earnest prayers,
To us mortals Here Below grant hope and mercy!

This ballad of the *tayffart* genre was collected in 1933 by Moha
u-Talb, one of Arsène Roux's informants, from a certain U-Shrif
of Tunfit (Ayt Bu Arbi sub-clan of the Ayt Shrad clan, Ayt Yahya
tribe), a famed former troubadour (*amdyaz*) well-known for his
fine voice and extensive knowledge.

This is a typically ambiguous, opaque poem highlighting the role of
the go-between, or messenger (*amazan*), in Amazigh poetry. Observe
the way the messenger decks himself out for his mission, donning
the Sufi-like garb of a wandering troubadour. The symbolism is also
significant, with references to the dove (incarnating woman), the
cave (where lovers consort) and water (associated with the act of

love). This particular messenger, like many others of his ilk, ends up taking his errand too seriously and falling in love with the woman to whom the amorous message is destined. Gullible as he is, though, the *amazan* is, in turn, outsmarted by his fickle lady-love. From the middle of the fourth stanza to the end of the fifth, the ballad becomes purely pedagogical as it dwells on female iniquity. The image of young trees that bow to the breeze, to which ancient tree-trunks remain impervious, portrays the comparative effects of passion on young and old, and is well-known to anybody familiar with Amazigh poetry, as enshrined in a famous *tamawayt* by Tawqrat Ult-Sokhman, the blind poetess of Aghbala, who died in about 1930:

> Thou visiteth not gnarl'd tree-trunks, O westerly breeze,
> Even high on the mount; would fain smite young leafy trees,
> Better fit to tremble with love's transports!

Ballad of Sheikh Aajami

O one and true God! Thine aid I do implore;
In this world guide my foot-steps, also in the Hereafter!
Thou who dost aid the cleric to write a letter canst grasp
My message, thou who dost lead the laden young camel!
O Lord! I beseech thee, O Sidna Muhand, divine intercessor,
Thou canst distinguish 'twixt light and darkness!
O Lord, I invoke thee in the name of the first Prophets,
Those who bore of Muhammad the Arab the white standards!
Fail me not, O Sidi Bu Zekri, patron saint of Meknes,
O great Ayssawi, of my ancestors the worthy successor!
Seek inspiration, O my muse, recount what hath come to pass;
Having woven the first thread, must now complete my task.

My tongue doth quiver, like the reed in waters
By westerly wind ruffl'd; like underground onion,
That will grow a second time, e'en when unearth'd.
Say it once more, O my muse, start our tale we must,
A single cross-bar sufficeth not to ensure the weaving.
Harm without cure on us did the Christian inflict!
Introduced us to tea and sugar our counsels to embroil!
Who faileth today to present well-garnished tea-tray,
Nor repast worthy of the name, succumbeth to dismay.
Few are they who can still offer platters with viands
Varied and plentiful, or hot water to cook choice dishes!

Harm without cure on us did the Christian inflict,
To wit, weapons most modern with unerring aim!
If the eye can see it, the bullet can reach it;
Mortal man thus smitten his innards doth spew!
O musket, art like the woman by her second wife upstag'd;
Art neglected and discarded, by Lebel rifle outclass'd!

I descended to Meknes, found there stacks of old guns
Without value; verily have we reach'd 'the end of time'!
No man wieldeth a musket, or e'en a single-shot rifle,
Just as the chicken's time doth come, so be it with old guns!
O one and true God! Thine aid I do implore!

This is another ballad of the *tayffart* genre, attributed to the
famous Sheikh Muhand Aajmi. It is a pre-Colonial text
belonging to the 1895–1905 period, recited by Assou ou Saïd to
Arsène Roux in Meknes, in about 1923.

Strong is the impression made on the poet by the arrival of the
Christians and their infallible new weapons; also by a series of
ground-breaking social changes that appear to announce 'the end
of time' (*xir zamam*), or at least the end of an epoch. Faith in God,
more than ever, remains the bard's ultimate refuge. The end of the
opening stanza reiterates an oft-repeated simile, comparing the
composition of poetry with spinning.

Feud at Ayt Naaman

Thy name I do first pronounce, O Prophet! Help me that I
May the reed straighten that groweth hard by the spring.
Thy name I do first pronounce, O Prophet, hallowed be
Thy name; from thy inspiration all words do emanate!
With sprightly step to Ayt Naaman did wend my way;
See me thou shalt anon, O girls who draw water!
'O maidens!' quoth he, 'what say the omens? What hath
Come to pass? Sooth to say, have only just arriv'd!'

Thus spake a girl: 'O flute-player, 'tis a day of mourning,
The villagers are too busy, unwanted visitors to welcome!'

On seeing the countenance of another girl he enjoin'd her
To cease scratching her cheeks, her beauty to preserve!
Eventually he prevail'd upon the girls to speak:
'There before thee standeth one of the hero's wives.
Heeding the bad news, Bugrin purchas'd gun-powder,
Prepar'd his fortifications to withstand a siege.
Like thunder sounded the guns, war-cries rent the air,
Brave men's red blood the thirsty soil did water!'

'Laamari did fall, he who was in my heart of hearts,
To whom God had granted mules and oxen aplenty!
Had he but kept his bed rather than face the foe…
Seven good men of Ayt Urtindi have fallen this day!
Since the sharif was traitorously slain at Mulay Driss,
The spring hath dried to the bone, yielding water no more!'
Meanwhile from Fez rose a sound of revelry by night,
As citizens danced *ahidus*; but where was the bride to be?

Fez is like unto a raging furnace, frequently by all and
Sundry fuelled; unbearable is thy heat, O flames!
Wast right well cook'd, O man from Bu Zemmur.
From the flame, however, lesser mortals shy away.
O Bu Hmara! Henceforth power is in thy hands,
As for Mulay Abd al-'Aziz his time is long past!
O Bu Hmara! O mighty sharif, raise high thine
Immaculate standards, O Lord, lead on to victory!
May the Prophet's name be sanctified, allow me,
O Lord, that peerless prayer to pronounce!

Again a ballad of the *tayffart* genre, this time attributed to Sheikh
Assu of the Ayt Sliman clan, Ayt Yahya region (Tunfit). This bard,
who is operating in the Middle Atlas, far from his home base, is
reputed to have died before the Protectorate period.

In the first stanza we have an example of pronominal permutation so typical of Berber poetry where, in full flight, the bard switches from first to third person, probably for dramatic effect. Given the references to pretender Bu Hamara's rebellion against Sultan Mulay Abd al-'Aziz, when for a short time he actually threatened the imperial capital of Fez, the poem probably dates to 1902–3. Otherwise, the poem relates one of many pointless, tragic feuds; in this case between Ayt Naaman *qayd* Bugrin Ahizun and rival Ayt Ndhir clans under Muhand u-Qessu, caïd of the Ayt Ayssa u-Brahim. As they scratch their cheeks in mourning, the Ayt Ndhir womenfolk blame events of this kind, in which many a good man dies for nothing, on the bad luck that dogs the clan since their recent betrayal to Sultan Mulay Hafid of the intriguer, sharif Sidi Muhand al-Kettani.

Ballad on love-sickness

A prayer to the Prophet, 'tis to the heart like honey,
Sweet utterances of Mulay Muhand, by the Lord refin'd!
To problems here below the Lord of the Heavens doth
Hold the key, He whose writ runneth large o'er worldly things!
To you I do appeal, O saints, where'er ye be – known
And unknown – grant me now favourable inspiration!
My burden shall I shoulder, O Lord, and shall to the clerics appeal,
Those providers of knowledge, that they may check my fall!
Setting one foot before the other, there's nothing finer,
But if thou stridest, be humble lest thou takest a tumble!
O wayfarer, when dost on a slope unthinkingly venture,
Shouldst thou slip, from God expect no succour!

Well then, who gave me the news I do now impart?
O ye that hear me, repeat what is said across the land!

May God have you in safe-keeping, O damsels,
'Tis the pleasure of beauty that thou offerest,
O Fadma, with those features I hold so dear!
When Fadma henna doth prepare, unerringly
Her thoughts turn to horses, tea-pots and fine glasses!
O Lord, this day since my awakening I do daydream,
Thinking of the spot where Fadma hath pitched her tent!
Dream not of the loved one, O troubadour, 'tis not good;
Will perforce to needless regrets and sorrow give rise!
A vision did I see – that by my side Fadma was lying,
Till at midday, with a start, melancholy awoke me!

As if I had my mother interr'd, tears course down my cheeks,
Love of dear ones e'er stronger be than worldly considerations!
O Lord, could I but knowledgeable cleric find, well versed in potions,
Love's shackles to shatter, I would unhesitatingly pay his due!
O unbridled passion for women that haunteth my heart, O cleric,
Remove it, I beseech thee, that I may from its bonds break free!
To consult a cleric I did go, he being of erudition renown'd,
Bade him prepare magic spells two, nay if need be three!
Quoth he: 'Verily, what is writ on paper, of fever will rid thee;
Upon love's melancholy, however, it doth remain powerless!'
Help cometh not from the Book; e'en though her love hath to
These dire straits reduced me, my succour can but come from Fadma!
Meanwhile, like a demented one, without breaking my fast, I
    wander through the encampment . . .

This ballad of the *tayffart n-tefsutt* genre is attributed to Sheikh Nbarsh u-
Muhand from Tazruft, Zawit Sidi Hamza, and was collected by Arsène
Roux in Lhajeb between 1914 and 1918.

Though to our Western minds, such literary fare may appear
irrelevant, rambling and redundant, by local standards it is a

consummate work of art. This eminently didactic poem portrays, as its main thread, the troubadour's predicament as he wanders through the land, in the time approved Sufi tradition, preaching to rural Amazigh communities by means of pedagogical poems, while his thoughts ever return to his lady love, Fadma of the beautiful countenance. The allusion to horse, tea-pot and fine glasses highlights their symbolic importance in love-making. The remaining lines are devoted to appeasing the Lord and his Prophet, whose power by far exceeds all worldly considerations. Yet, ironically, after vainly resorting to the local cleric (*ttalb*), even God ultimately proves powerless to find a cure for the melancholy that holds the troubadour in thrall.

Unhappy plight of the troubadour

O one and only God, your name I do first pronounce,
Guide my footsteps Here Below and in the Hereafter!
Would that I could my brain remove, become demented,
Alas! Must ever wander through the land – 'tis my lot!
Could the tents of the world but verse compose, misfortune
Would prevail, O ye tambourine-players and dancers!
Should we to chanting songs our lives solely devote,
Milk would remain un-churn'd, fruit on the trees unpick'd!
Without cattle on the pastures, rife would be poverty,
O ye white-clad ones, song and dance is mere frivolity!

Delude thyself not, the muse barely elevates the spirit,
Happy that thou be to remain in thy sheep-fold on the hill!
Should wealth be thy goal, go summon kith and kin;
Let them raise flocks of sheep and elevate castle great!
Sooth to say, shalt thereof gain but little profit,

Thy path wilt be with thistles strewn – mark my word!
Woe is me, my fields lie unplough'd, neglected! O poem,
Thou art my livelihood; give me my drum and flute!
I preach on barren ground; neither goat, nor sheep do
Raise, with those of neighbouring herds to compete!

I have observed God's work, before me plainly visible,
O my fated destiny, no turning back, thou art written!
This year, like the one that went before, no stallions have I
Ridden, nor mules purchas'd, nor houses built.
Loth am I with friends and sweetheart to part,
However, 'tis written – what must be must be!
I would fain not face hot trails, O flat country!
E'en less water and bitter cold or bone-piercing winds!
O Intercessor, O father of Fatima, thy protection I do crave!

This ballad of the *tamdyazt* genre was recited to Arsène Roux in
Lhajeb, between 1914 and 1918, by Sheikh Nbarch of Tazruft,
Zawit Sidi Hamza.

It is a monologue on the troubadour's miserable existence, con-
demned as he is to wander across the face of the land to earn his
living, clad in rags and worn sandals, his face exposed willy-nilly to
wind, sun and rain. A picaresque existence such as this obviously
affords little time to tend flocks or vegetable-patch, making him
totally dependent on others. Yet paradoxically given his illiteracy,
because of his degree of oral erudition, the *amdyaz* may be
considered a genuine rural intellectual, a character able to wield
considerable influence on his society.

Battle of Tazuggwart

Bring us tidings, speak, O mouth!
Criticise not, forget not one word.
We are by the French most hard press'd,
They took Buwaanan; resistance prov'd
Hopeless; they destroy'd thee, proud Bshara.
All hope is lost, they are beyond Dahra,
They have reach'd Budnib and still advance.
O Budnib, hast become the world's centre
Where, as Muslim and Christian do battle,
The ground trembles from myriad hooves.
O Budnib, this year's battle is the worst.

The Christian set fire, defil'd our holy places.
O saintly leader, didst thou not see them?
Ayt Gir and Ayt Ayssa defeated, towards the
Hills did flee, sought refuge on the mountain-top.
Wage Holy war, O Muslims; see the Christians,
Those infidels, who prepare to march towards us.
Will take thy homeland from thee, will force
Thee to betray, will seek to dislodge thee.
However, will come the day when Islam's voice
Shall strike the guard upon the rampart; then
Shall be slain all Christians!

Shalt say: 'Our time hath come, O Berbers,
Anon shall thine enemies be vanquish'd!'
At dawn towards us the Christians march'd,
From their cannon huge havoc unleash'd.
At the war-camp, many who heard the guns' distant
Thunder turn'd and fled their hearts full of dread.

Some lost their way, climb'd towards the peaks,
Others 'cross the plain did roam, rack'd by thirst.
All was lost: tents, bag, baggage and cooking-pot,
Dire defeat did we suffer at the Christians' hands!

Long is the road to Tazuggwart's fateful field
Where by the hundred our fighters were felled!
Many driven to folly, e'en death did disdain,
A few more days stay'd rooted to the spot.
O madmen, art not bereft of life and death?
Our destiny is in the hands of God on high!
The wealthy man hiding in a wooden chest
Can do naught to avert the hand of Fate!
O cousins who fought at Tazuggwart, forget
It not till the day our women rise up in arms!

Here is another ballad of the *tamdyazt* genre, attributed to
a famous troubadour, Sheikh Mulay Aomar of Tazruft
(Zawit Sidi Hamza), on the south side of Jbel Ayyachi. It was
collected by Arsène Roux at Lhajeb between 1914 & 1918.

This poem refers to a disastrous defeat, in which the resistance
fighters failed in an attempt to capture the French fort at Budenib in
1908. A large force of Berber horsemen was involved, hundreds of
whom were slaughtered by machine-gun and artillery fire. Such was
the psychological impact of this disaster that never again would
Amazigh fighters resort to mass cavalry charges over open ground.
Observe the poet's defiant attitude; in his hearts of hearts he feels
that one day the tables will be turned on the Christian.

Battle of El-Herri

Pray to the Prophet! As for the caitiff Christian who
Warneth not the Lord when he oppresseth his brother;
Deed such as this is as natural as ascending Mount Arafa.
Tell me, good folk, of the sinner who prayeth not,
Neither generosity displayeth, nor tithes giveth
To the mosque; whence can come his salvation?
Believers fittingly must raise their progeny, the holy
Koran teach them. Would that I could safely come to ye,
And greet ye, O good people in whom I put my trust!

O Mulay Buazza of the white horses, who crosseth the land,
May the Master of Taqeddust grant me safe passage!
Sidi Ali Hassayn, be thou ever my guardian protector; thy
Hospitality shall I meekly implore, wretch that I am!
O saints, should ye betray me, such would be my disarray,
That highway would become sole refuge to this poor minstrel!
To El-Herri didst thou go, sojourn'd in hamlet small,
The villagers had sown what little grain they possess'd.
May God upon the Zayani shower his blessing!
Hallow'd be the Lord who purifieth the great ones!

From yon hills did descend the destructive Rumi,
Ere break of day, ere we'd said our prayers – the felon!
Would fain deny it, yet our camels, mules, treasure were
Captur'd. The chiefs' wives suffered the doves' fate, as
When falcons with crooked talons upon their prey swoop!
Mimuna n-Hmad's life-blood was upon the cushions spill'd.
My tears flow unchecked as for Mahjuba and Tihihit I mourn.
The wicked Ba Hassin and Umar, their blades sharpen'd,
Struck you blows so pitiless, O Zayani, those nephews
Who dishonourably did their anger vent upon you!

Classic Oral Poetry from the Middle Atlas 33

Thus the French officer, after his inaction of early years,
Did by night with the Unbelievers stealthily pounce!
Messawd, the Lieutenant, indeed was forgiven,
For among the hills leaving the metal thunderers!
Up at the pass were you left stranded, O great guns!
Like a young camel abandon'd by unworthy masters!
Seven pieces of artillery stuck in the mud like sticks,
Expos'd to sun and rain, for a week did remain!
The day they fetch'd the colonel's stinking corpse,
His pot-belly upon the ground the guts did spill!

Tarry a while, thou that leavest; whither goest thou?
Uninformed was Qayd Jilali of these grievous happenings.
Many a Moroccan fought in the battle, direly did suffer,
Deeply and tragically was Muha u-Hemmu aggriev'd!
May God upon my progeny malediction pronounce if he
Alloweth the Christian to invest Khenifra ere we meet the
French in the field, and whiche'er way the battle goeth!
Quoth Bu Seqqur: 'He who cameth his thirst for to
Slake, my waters' erstwhile purity fail'd to find.
Lo, 'tis with gore that the river is redden'd!'
This place most sinister doth awake memories
Of carrion rent by eagles' beaks, and jackals
Devouring corpses! May God bless ye, O Imazighen,
For the sword blows struck against the Senegalese!

This ballad of the *tayffart Imejriyat* genre, relating an important event,
was collected by Arsène Roux from Muha u-Heddu u-Amr, a poet living
at Lqbab (1932–4). Some doubt exists as to the authenticity of this
amdyaz, who, at any rate did not belong to the Zawit Sidi Hamza
'school'. This is clear from the identity of the saints from whom he
invokes protection – Mulay Buazza, renowned twelfth century Middle
Atlas marabout, and Sidi Ali Hassayn of the Imhiwash line of *igurramn*,
referred to here as 'the master of Taqeddust'.

This poem refers to an event on 14 November 1914 when, acting on information supplied by two Berbers, the nephews of Muha u-Hemmu (with a grievance against him), a French column under Colonel Laverdure staged a pre-dawn attack on the Zayan chief's camp near El-Herri, south of Khenifra. After plundering his tents and killing some of his wives, the French began a fighting retreat over ten miles of broken ground back to Khenifra outpost. They never got there. From all points of the compass Berber fighters converged on them, forced them to abandon their artillery, killed most of their officers and left the Senegalese rank and file, making up 90% of the French column, to fight their way home as best they could. Many were slaughtered along the oleander-lined banks of Oued Bu Seqqur. It was the French army's worst ever defeat in North Africa.

Conquest of Morocco (I)

Thy name I first pronounce, O Muhammad, grant me among
Thy servants honourable rank; may his name be prais'd!
The Christian at Amghas did barracks build, occupied
Aguray and Amekla; hath verily taken over our world!
By Mulay Hassan's residence and amidst our turret'd
Mosques, the swine hath rais'd outlandish buildings!
O red-wall'd city, O Dar Debbibagh! The sultan's power be
Destroy'd, everywhere Christians do strut and swagger!
Wear mourning for our cities: Fez, Meknes, Aguray, Sefru,
Tabadut! The Christian hath our destruction encompass'd!
Fez, Meknes and Casablanca are now home to the swine,
Could we but make the raven's plumage turn white again?!

O Muha u-Seyd, do thou strive against the foe, strike boldly!
Wherefore hast thou terminated thy *jihad* against the Rumi?

O Muha u-Seyd, rider of russet-red steed, hast all the assets,
Yet makest light of bullets, and artillery shells that strike us!
And thou, O Zayani, against the invader fight the good fight,
Thou hast modern weapons aplenty to match the swine!
What use thy big guns, thy numberless horses, O Zayani?
Though didst the Rumi vanquish; what of thy victory at El-Herri?
What of your halls of reception, your carv'd cedar ceilings,
Or the blue tiles that adorn your walls, O cowardly chiefs?!
O men of Arfa and Arekla, behold the white-wash'd spring,
Place of your ablutions; now by the Christian defil'd!
Passing through Azru did descry Tit Lahsen; Christians drank
Of its waters; forsooth, 'the end of time' is upon us!

Weep, O Tabadut, wear mourning, O Bujaad and thou, Azru!
Weep, O Aguray, verily hath the Christian depriv'd ye!
Wives sorely do weep at Tabadut, at Aguray, a third in prison.
O Lord, do thou assist Berber women in their hour of need!
From sunrise to sunset the soldiers conduct their operations,
A hail of rifle bullets falls in lieu of wonted spring showers!
One his lorry rideth, the other his sword draweth, a third one
With Lebel rifle doth wreak devastation throughout the land!
One with shells crusheth all before him; the other's machine-gun
Death doth spit; e'en the flowers disappear when they're gone!
The proud standards of Islam have fallen to earth, the foul
Christian's flag waveth in the wind; hath our world conquer'd!
Swept away as before a flood, are gone our state and religion;
In the Christian camp, one dead officer is by two easily replaced!

A ballad of the *tayffart* genre, author unknown, collected by Arsène Roux,
probably in Lhajeb, between 1914 and 1924.

After early successes against the French, at Qsiba (1913) and El-
Herri (1914), Muha u-Seyd and Muha u-Hemmu Zayani, like other

traditional Moroccan leaders, have remained somewhat inactive. In the face of this foreign invader, his modern weapons and over-whelming resources, the poet displays a certain sense of patriotism and emphasizes the sense of shame that pervades the Moroccan nation. Coming from a reputedly uncouth highland Berber (thus visualized even today by the urban *glitterati*), this sentiment speaks volumes for the patriotism of the Imazighen.

Conquest of Morocco (II)

Inspire me that I may sing of the Christian!
Many of our valiant fighters hath he laid low!
Hath Sahara conquer'd, taken Tulal, Atlantic Plain;
Bashnu, too, hath fallen; a fort overlooketh Budnib!
Sefru, Lhajeb and Aguray are also taken, whilst
Our womenfolk of their veils have been stripp'd!
O Fez, behold new buildings, the sacred spring defil'd.
Harm without cure on us did inflict the Christian!
Weapons they do possess, unerring be their aim.
How can we dance *ahidus* when the Christian is nigh?
Hath the drum taken, Berber women to his tune do dance!

What hard times are these! The returning Mecca pilgrim hath
His castle embellish'd; doth trade with Jews in the market!
Lo! From your bolt-holes you now emerge, O profiteers!
What double-dealing is afoot, O Allal, and you, Hassan!
Pray tell me, whence cometh these ill-gotten gains?
As for Lhou and Aabbi, hollow do ring their denials!
Flow uncheck'd, O tears, to sin is the cavern devoted,
E'en in the town centre prostitutes ply their trade!
Seyd hath wife repudiated for consorting with soldiers!

As for Hmad, e'en greater dishonour on him lieth,
His daughter disports herself 'mid soldiers' tents!
Small wonder, ever meretricious was her conduct!

This ballad of the *tayffart* genre, attributable to a famous
amdyaz calld Jeddi, was collected at Lhajeb in 1916 by Arsène
Roux from Heddu u-Rezzuq of the Ayt Hassi u-Seyd (Ayt Ndhir).

Here the conquest of Morocco is seen through yet another bard's
eyes. After the habitual catalogue of captured towns, the poet
demonstrates how heavily the dishonour of the Moroccan people
lies on the land: Muslims taking advantage of newfound wealth to
trade with Christians and Jews; women unveiled, dancing before
Frenchmen, or disporting themselves with soldiers. This last point
really emphasizes the moral debâcle, bearing in mind that the most
intimate sanctuary, or *hurm*, implying the very honour of this
Muslim population, resides in its women-folk.

Conquest of Morocco (III)

In thy name this poem I do commence, O Lord and
God's Envoy, when summoned by Death's Angel!
Mercy on me, O Prophet, O great intercessor,
I no longer pray nor fast; do neglect thee, O mosque!
Ever anxious to please, am by others ignor'd,
Yet 'twas written; O hearth-stone, be thou my succour!
O son of Adam, heavy the burden that thou bearest!
O stock-breeder! Farmer doth with muezzin consort.
Paradise will be his lot, admittance shall not be denied!
Forsooth! Goodness incarnate is the farmer!
For their well-being ant and bird do seek sustenance.

Wouldst have some learning? Do thou to the cleric repair,
Shall the scroll unroll, explain words' hidden meaning.

Hence from me, unworthy utterance, inspiration cometh from God;
Should I of litigation be fond, must acquire learning to hold my own!
Behold, the Christian hath come, for his automobiles roads doth
    build;
To prevent tongues wagging this reality must be fac'd!
Aeroplanes made of iron nails the highest heavens do reach.
Behold the lightning flashes of his big guns,
Sad be thy plight, O Islam, of guiding light depriv'd!
Mistaken art thou, O sun, powerless do we remain,
Having implor'd the Lord, to Mecca our prayer did fly!
When I hear the muezzin's call my faith melteth away.
Between men brotherhood is absent. Solidarity didst thou say?
By the Christian aided and abetted, deceit lurketh in men's hearts!
Pooh! Justice hath departed – no recourse for wretch or orphan;
E'en the passer-by of his goods shall be depriv'd!
If thou hast truck with the Rumi, count thyself unlucky!
O youngster, thy behaviour of rottenness doth savour,
When problems loom, solve them ye must; ill chosen
Were our young men's weapons to combat the Christian!

This is a teaching ballad of the *tayffart n-ttuhid* genre, attributed to Sheikh
Lahsen of Ayt Izdeg, from whom it was collected by Arsène Roux at
Lhajeb, some time between 1914 and 1924.

This poem shows a highly critical perception of the adverse effects
of the Christian occupation and their defective legal system, the
focus being on the Godlessness that stalks the land, tantamount to
a total moral and spiritual breakdown of Moroccan society.

Ayt Ndhir ballad on the Christian

In thy name I commence my poem, O Sidi Muhammad,
Sweet are thy words, O Prophet from whom I seek inspiration!
In thy name I commence my poem, O Almighty God,
Who hath created moon, stars and sun – long may he last!
In thy name I commence my poem, O Almighty God,
Centre of the universe and of bountiful harvest the harbinger!
After saying your name, O Muhammad, smoothly do flow my
Words, 'coz 'tis bliss indeed with thee to converse, O Prophet!
Watch over wayward children that do religion neglect,
Islam is indeed laid aside when the mosque standeth empty!

Wherefore this further harassment, O Rumi invader!
He dominateth the land, his law imposeth, heavy be his hand!
Whither are ye gone, O saints, clerics and valiant marksmen?
Believers admit with downcast eye that the Holy War is no more!
O Sidi Ali Bennasr, patron saint of marksmen, lead on to war!
O huntsmen, 'tis worthier game than the lion that ye track today!
Thou that hearest this tale, mark well my words, ask Believers that
They pardon me – may God keep the peace 'twixt them and me!
Reflecting upon our ancestors' words, their warning did recall,
From father to son transmitted: 'One day shall the Christian come!'

Of our destiny did take note: who our neighbour should be, which
Booty I was to yield, O Almighty, all things by thee ordain'd!
Have no confidence in the Christian. Act with him like at harvest
    time:
Once measur'd and gather'd in, crops to the merchant are swiftly
    sold!
With flame and thunder the Rumi cannon did outmatch the
    cartridges

Of the Muslims' puny rifles, by the French all now confiscated!
O stallions, gone is bravery; should one of our young men mount
His steed, he rides unarm'd; truthfully is the spice of life departed!
Our rifles confiscated, O Berbers, for all of you, the sound of steel is
Silent, honour is gone. To an alien form of logic do you now react!

This day do Christians oppress us, they keep watch o'er us; O Islam,
Fate is unkind, should somebody raise a finger, is forthwith
        imprison'd!
Quiet is the land now that justice settles our disputes – 'tis no longer
Violence, or money, that I can now keep to be spent on pleasure!
Should the French depart, our caravans would be by robbers
        waylaid,
The hawker stripp'd of his wares unless prepar'd dearly his life to
        sell!
Observe, O ye men and women, that injustice be gone, the ruffian's
Word is law no more – o'er us doth captain Nivelle keep watch!

This genre of ballad is known as *zedday* among the Ayt Ndhir (Beni Mtir),
a major Middle Atlas Amazigh tribe. It was collected by Arsène Roux at
Lhajeb (1914–18) and the Berber text was revised by one of his
informants, a certain Hussa u-Muha from Azru, in 1962. I translated the
poem with help from Labha Elasri and Ayesha Azzawi (Ifrane, 2001).

The preamble is addressed to God and his saints, and is followed by
the usual catalogue of woes at the failure of Morocco's warriors to
stand up against the invader. Apparent regret that matters of honour
can no longer be settled by the time-honoured use of steel is
countered in the final stanza where the bard appears resigned to his
country's fate, and please, at least, that the rule of law, in the shape
of the *Affaires Indigènes* officer sitting in his office (*lbiru*), has come
to inland Morocco.

A collection of short poems on the
Middle Atlas campaign

O white war-horse, neighieth not with delight! Slain be
Thy master; could I but to the tomb have follow'd him!

Farewell, O country of mine, I have forsaken thee!
Hath arriv'd he who hateth Muhammad the Prophet!

The Christian hath come, built outposts amidst Zaer hills;
O'er Fez city flieth his flag, in his grip the land doth hold!

O Prophet, hast thou not thy sandals remov'd, the better to escape?!
I too seek safety in flight; thus do we share the same predicament!

At Tabadut have the *Joyeux* built an outpost, dug ditches deep,
Rais'd corner-towers; shame on ye who did not fight them!

Praise be to God! Those unfortunate Ayt Myill tremble with fear,
When they hear that the French *qebtan* hath reach'd Jbal Hayyan!

O Bu Madel, unworthy camp site by the mujahideen chosen,
Wilt prove their undoing; famous shall be this year for their
Sacrifice. Was it not rash to enter those unknown marshes?
Sooth to say, had heard of big guns the thunder!

Should I make war, should I kiss the Frenchman's hand,
Should I thus renounce poetry and beautiful women?

O *qebtan*, O general, this country be thine since to
Defend it we were powerless! Do with it as you will!

The Ayt Abdi have climb'd up the mountain; grass shall be
Their daily fare; as for me am but a prisoner of the *qebtan*!

Mules I still possess bag and baggage to transport, also
Tea to drink and wheat to keep the wolf from the door!
I will remain among those who have retain'd their pride!

Thus spake Terwillal hill: 'Have espoused a wild boar.
O Hemmu u-Aamr! Go lurk in yon hills' remotest cranny,
Bitter cold doth better become thee than Christians' tyranny!'

I crave your bounty, O Rumi, being from my tent-brothers
        separated!
Lord, may after glory the master of big guns yearn, may he take
        with
Him his artillery up into the high hills!

O folk, drink of the water wherein perish'd the donkey,
O ye that do surrender, with misfortune shall be smitten!

Not on your life! Why drink of those polluted waters?
Fetch pure water from Bu Wferra and Ayn Sihand springs!

O cavaliers that provide escort for the officer Desjobert,
Wherefore do ye disobey the Prophet's teachings?!

As I pass'd above Aguray, Mennahu's voice did hear,
She was calling to me, yet by her side stood Desjobert!

Rumour had it that Desjobert had taken wife;
Then we discover'd that Mennahu was his bride!

Verily, I tell you, kind be the Christian; without
Him orphans and widows injustice would suffer!

How canst say that? Were he good, he would not
Have push'd our holy leaders into the sea;
'Tis the crime of which he standeth accus'd!

Ayn Lkhil spring thus did speak: 'Of the Zayan be
Not afeard, so long as standeth Ahushar fortress!'

Hardy fighters be the Zayan! Should they have weapons
With which to smite the swine, each day would threaten them!

The enemy hath pass'd Boujaad, crossed Tafudayt hills,
Soon, I fear, O Master of the White Towers, he shall reach thee!

O Sheikh Muhand, O master of the White Towers, 'tis because
Of your misdeeds past, O Zayani, that the Rumi pursueth thee!

Khenifra's empty houses are of mewing cats the abode;
Torn asunder be my heart, unexpected tears do flow!

Among the hills Fadma doth weep. Thus spake she:
'O Aqqa Miami, proud cavalier, gone be all Khenifra's
Inhabitants; broken the doors, their houses stand empty!'

Khenifra, mistress of a thousand horses, didst thou not say:
'Hardy the Ayt Lburj until the French officer smote them?!'

Thus spake Khenifra: 'Painful be our plight;
Who shall rid us of the stinking Senegalese!'

Was nois'd abroad news of Khenifra's capture by Berger;
Small wonder – exceedingly unwarlike were its defenders!

How pleasant the plain doth seem on this day of destruction;
Should you chase me, O Berger, shall in the hills find refuge!

Well, Awzzin, leave now this village, occupied by Berger and
His aeroplanes! Consort, for all I care, with the *Joyeux*, those
Wearers of *képis*; may they take you with them a-soldiering!

To all who can hear him Berger thus doth speak:
'O Hussa, wherefore do thy guns remain silent?!'

Thus spake Bu Hayati to Tizi Uqellal: 'Whither didst ye go,
O people of Umm Rabiaa? Were ye not facing the Christian?
Ignominiously did Aqqa flee without firing a bullet!'

Thus did Bu Hayati hill speak to Aqellal pass: 'Where is Hassan's
Cannon; why fireth he not on the invaders who invest Khenifra?'

To crown a sad day, Hassan and Amharoq,
The unspeakable chiefs, whiled the time away in futile skirmishes!

I can now expect but dishonourable chastisement,
Shall a mule-driver be with Hassan and Amharoq!

Like buzzards the Imehzan hover o'er the hills,
The Ayt Ishaq too, our villages invest!
O death! What other alternative remaineth?

These are miscellaneous snatches of verse of the *izli* and *tamawayt* genre,
dealing with the Middle Atlas campaign, collected, for the most part, by
Arsène Roux at El Hajeb during the 1914–18 war.

The action centres in these poems centres on Khenifra, the Zayan
capital, and its environs. The central figures are Muha u-Hemmu
Zayani, referred to as the 'Master of the White Towers', and Captain
Berger, *bershi* to the Berbers, author of a biography on the famous
Zayan chieftain. The bard regrets the manner of Khenifra's taking,
the present condition of the derelict town, inefficiently defended by
Zayan tribesmen now lurking in the hills. In fact, there is a general
feeling of shame at the poor performance put up by Middle Atlas
fighters. In contrast, some hardier spirits obviously contemplate
living on grass and holding out 'til the bitter end in the cold hills.
Even Muha u-Hemmu's sons Hassan, Amharoq and Hussa, coming
from a long line of warriors, possessors of a battery of antiquated
cannon, have failed to bring them into play and are generally

censured for their lack of activity. Of the other characters, Awzzin is a well-known courtesan; Desjobert, known locally as *zubair*, is the Native Affairs officer at Lhajeb recently married to Mennahu, a local beauty. The *képi*-wearing *Joyeux*, their ranks made up of convicted criminals lucky enough to escape a prison sentence, constitute the very dregs of the French Army. Bu Hayati and Tizi Uqellal are conspicuous features in the landscape surrounding Khenifra. The Imehzan refers to Muha u-Hemmu Zayani and his family.

Ballad on the Zayan and Ayt Ndhir

Do first pronounce thy name, in my distress help me;
Assist not the human race, 'twould be but time wasted!
O great sheikh, O Sidi u-Telha, thee or thy son,
Against mine enemies erect defensive barrier!
O holy city of Mecca, thy founders I do implore;
Pray heed my call, to the encampment bear my burden!
O charitable ones, ye that provide help and protection,
Can ye not save me, O worshippers of the true God?!
Speak, O mouth, inspiration and fresh tidings bring!
See how like the spinner the bard his yarn doth spin!

Avast, ye standards, by treachery cast to the ground!
O fellow-countryman, where shall I commence my tale?
Have almost forgotten, O Khenifra, what hath befallen thee?
Did say to myself: 'No doubt, as before hath she remain'd!'
Gladly imagin'd that till dawn would in revelry indulge!
As the gates drew near could almost catch the scent of kif!
I stood still before the gate; the sentry did challenge me.
Was stunned into silence, nor could he find words.
'Prithee, my Lord!' said I, 'answer me truthfully!'
'Speak!' quoth he, 'What bringeth you here?'

'Dost that doughty fighter, Sheikh Muha u-Hemmu,
Still provide subsidy for wandering bards such as me?'

'Look you, Muha u-Hemmu, the swordsman you mention,
In Khenifra no longer resideth; shalt find but the Christian!
His son Buazza, as an officer with the French doth serve;
The rogue shamefully clotheth himself in girls' robes!
Cardeth no wool, yet doth raid the resistance fighters!
How can Hussa in his hillside fastness still hold out? His
Father dead, like his brothers, shall soon join the French!
The Imehzan like leaderless cattle do behave;
Where be gone their chiefs? Think nought but of retreat!
The Imehzan, like a proud white war-horse with panniers
Equipped, no longer to the mustering place repairs!
The Imehzan are little better than a sterile orchard;
Once the fences are down, is given over to the herd!

The Imehzan are like an estate, whereof the numerous
Inheritors squabble, each one aspiring to obtain his share!
The Imehzan are like a drought-stricken pasture;
Dry indeed the spring that made grass and flowers grow!
The Imehzan set but little store by their homeland;
They act like the wiseacres who say: 'I told you so!'
Could the Imazighen, just for once, show a united front,
Would not be oblig'd their spouses to abandon to soldiers!'
If a guest cometh, watch him well; ne'er smileth
Ere the tea-pot singeth atop the brazier!
However, should mint and tea be lacking, so
Long as there be kus-kus and meat, despair not!

Speak, O mouth, inspiration and fresh tidings bring,
See how like the spinner the bard his yarn doth spin!
Ayt Ndhir tribe what of your past valour? Hast forsaken

The path of glory; of your heyday nothing doth remain!
Art like the flower that withereth at the first frost; like the
Sheep that overmuch grazeth – leaveth naught but droppings!
Like a herd of lambs ye behave with the Christian;
Should one rebellion show, him doth the Rumi punish!
Forc'd labour your reward shall be, O former warriors,
Gone your pride, O ye that now break stones!
Of wages or other reward, none; nor little thanks!
Even less in the way of encouragement!

The Christian in his wooden birds ruleth the skies;
In telegraph wires that cross the land his strength resideth!
When you muster for work, Driss the foreman, passeth
The word: 'Should you see a Christian give him a *bujjur*!
Shake his hand; when he walketh forward, follow behind;
Shall with my stick strike you and teach you manners!'
O God, thy name I do first pronounce, please help me,
Assist not the human race, 'twould be but time wasted!

This ballad of the *tamdyazt* genre, attributable to the Sheikh
Nbarsh of Tazruft, was collected by Arsène Roux between 1917
and 1923. For the sake of coherence the poem has been
divided by the translator into stanzas of slightly unequal length.

Again, the poet establishes the parallel between his art and that of
the spinner. This poem reveals the still-militant state of mind
among Berbers in around 1920 on the Saharan side of the Great
Atlas, compared to the situation obtaining in the Middle Atlas
where the resistance was on its last legs. As an *amdyaz*, the sheikh
has always been sure of a warm welcome from the great Zayan chief,
who regularly slaughtered several sheep to entertain travellers of
that standing, so he hopes to find him as usual in his capital,
Khenifra. Muha u-Hemmu, however, defiant till the end, has retired

towards the heights, his death actually reported at the skirmish of Azlag n-Tzemmurt on 27 March 1921. The theme of dishonour is strong, through an allusion to fallen standards and the crowning indignation of seeing the Berber women-folk as playthings for the soldiery. Worse still, the Imehzan, feudal lords of the great Zayan tribe, formerly proud fighters, appear more concerned by material matters than the defence of their home turf. Indeed, hedging their bets against the immediate future, two of the Zayani's sons, Hassan and Amharoq, have already gone over to the French. A third, Buazza, is shortly to die in an affray with the resistance fighters of the Melwiya. As for their Ayt Ndhir neighbours, pacified since 1914 and tamely kowtowing to the French, most have to come to terms with the unpaid labour system of *corvées*, thus becoming, according to the terminology of those who still held out in the Atlas, mere *ayt bujjur* ("sons of those that say 'Bonjour!'"; viz. those who have made their peace with the invader).

Ballad of moral teaching

Thou hast neither father nor mother, yet thou
Comest first! Uplift our spirits lest they fall!
Forward, O inspiration, let my story unfold,
God is all powerful, mortal man can do naught.
Cunning must I be to smell thee, O incense!
Troubl'd my head, giddy thoughts inhabit me.
As if I were with blindness stricken, in a deep well
Fallen, from kith and kin can expect no succour.
Unless Fadma or Ittu to my hands apply henna,
From no quarter may I crave assistance!
I consort with damsels, wielders of knives so sharp,
Woe is me, hand or finger will easily be sever'd!

Thrust not perchance thy finger in a cavity
Lest the venomous viper bite thee!
Evil existeth, stint it must 'fore my door;
Will surely visit the man that biteth the dust!
The traveller in far lands his goal doth achieve,
True Muslim resign'd to his fate must be!
Hold thy peace, let sleeping dogs lie,
Make light of insults, be of naught afeard!
O loud-mouth'd one, much aggriev'd shalt be if
Deservedly censor'd for bad language – 'tis a fact!
I hold my peace, walking with downcast eyes,
To others extend a hand, just be our laws!
In the sheikh's absence, e'en should I be
Stealing from a sheep-fold, an oath can swear!

Pay the co-jurors, there the matter shall stand,
Unless he doth the plaintiff's case uphold!
Am loth before the French officer my case to state;
At his door I hesitate, e'en forget my complaint!
Am weighed down by tribulations, of which
Frequent quarrels with Laabisha, my lov'd one!
Minor misdemeanour is now by law settl'd;
In patience rather than violence the solution lieth!
Today, what hath the evil-doer gain'd?
I accuse him, he can the charges answer;
Keep a pure heart, receive no bribes!
God knows! Be patient, just be our laws!
He who holdeth his tongue feareth naught,
Fret not thyself, scummy be excessive talk!

A ballad of the *tamdyazt n-ttuhid* type concerning moral
teaching about the true understanding of religion and
divine unity (*ttuhid*). Collected some time between 1914

and 1924 by Arsène Roux at Lhajeb from the famous
Sheikh Nbarsh of Tazruft, who used to say, '*da-ntwessa
medden*' ('we provide people with moral teaching').

Note the interesting remarks condemning the former practice of
resorting to bribes or violence to solve one's disputes, especially
the institution of collective oath-swearing, where the accused was
required to summon twenty or so co-jurors (*imgillan*) to exonerate
himself from blame. In earlier days, sheep-rustling could pass as a
relatively minor offence in a society where robbery involving an
element of risk, was regarded with favour. Under the French,
Moroccans were exhorted to rely on the decisions of the judiciary,
seen on the whole as fair, contrary to a more critical view
expounded on a similar topic in the previous poem.

Appeal to Sidi Mah

O Sidi Mah, thine aid I do implore!
O *agurram*, where hast thou been?
Thy young men nowhere to be seen!
In God's name go forth with thy *harka*,
That we may descend upon the plain.
Let them come if any warriors remain!
People in the know do claim that
The man with the *képi* is losing heart.
The Senegalese are ready to depart.
Of supplies the enemy is depriv'd!
No more guns, no more cartridges.
Sunken ships lie on Ocean's floor.
O young men, onwards to war!
Onwards to attack enemy outposts!

Stand steadfast despite the shells.
We'll capture the officer's horse,
We'll capture the French fort.
O warriors of Zawit Ahansal,
Come, conquer the Christian,
That in peace I may sleep again!

This is a fragment of an oral ballad, probably from Ayt Messad, Azilal. It was collected by Monsieur Coliac, interpreter at the Azilal outpost.

The renowned saint (*agurram*) Sidi Mah galvanised resistance against the French in the Central High Atlas region from his mountain sanctuary at Zawit Ahansal in the 1920–3 period, to which this poem belongs. Here, the poet urges the saint to march to victory against the French with his *harka* ('armed group') of mountain fighters, as the enemy is believed to be weakening in its resolve.

Ballad from Ayt Yahya

O one and true God, I beg of thee, please help me do,
In this world Here Below as in the Hereafter!
Help me along the way that I may my destination reach!
Your protection I do implore, O patron saint of hunters!
From this impious world banish heinous injustice,
To guide my footsteps send not the treacherous
Black-plum'd raven, but the white-wing'd dove!
O Lord! O Sidi Bu Ali, grant me thy protection,
Thou who dost rule over wind-ruffl'd ocean!

Whither would ye go, O footsteps? Peradventure
Towards my unhappy grave, that is not of this world?

Verily do my friends partake of choice viands,
Even though unseemly to me this may be.
A man most vile did eat his neighbour's share, then
Shut him out, saying: 'Be gone, I know thee not!'
Deed fit to turn the raven's plumage grey, the
Unspeakable one having eaten his neighbour's share!
Failure to present ritual tea-tray with glasses
On grounds of poverty, is but poor hospitality!
Hot water is for hands to wash before a choice meal,
'Tis not meet to serve a dish other than kuskus with meat.

Give thanks to Muhammad, O ye that receive his bounty!
Now please, release my mouth, that I may tell my tale!
Succour me, O Lord, on my dying day,
Cold from the Hereafter doth tickle my toes!
This cold slowly climbeth to my knees as I lie
Prone, like a tree-trunk by a wood-cutter fell'd!
Four of them carry me; here are two others
Busy digging the grave wherein I am fated to lie!
They are now seven as they sew the winding-sheet;
Says one: ' 'Tis but a short corpse, do as you see fit!'
One's opinion is worthless compar'd to God's.
Help me, O Lord, as thou hast always done!

I can feel my feet no longer, nor my hands,
Of mat or bed-clothes have I none.
My belly rent open by the grave-diggers,
I lie by flames and vipers surrounded!
In the Hereafter, 'tis a different set of rules,
No need for fines or oath-swearing to solve litigation!
To survive, grasp the bridle of your brother's mule,
Every man doth but reap what he hath sown!
Uninvited, at my funeral shall Death's Angel appear,

Then with sharp teeth shall drag me under ground,
Will dig deep my grave, sufficient earth for to find,
Then with pincers my interment shall finish!

As I journey'd on the road to Fez a caravan did espy,
And stopped to inquire whence those travellers came.
Their leader, one of ours, speaking full sadly,
With many a tear did thus give answer:
'Brother, be thou our guide; retrace thy footsteps,
Shalt otherwise be waylaid, unruliness is rife in the land!'
Happiness hath the Atlantic Plain forsaken, my friends!
He who hath business at home let him enjoy life!
With a cart did I wend my lonesome way from the ocean,
Cross'd the plain and climbed towards the hills of Fazaz.
Telephone lines ascend the slopes to Lhajeb and Aguray,
They make for Sefru. O Berber women, the Atlantic Plain
    is lost!'

To the Qarawiyin mosque did I journey and to Jbel Zerhun too;
The Koran read no more, the Christian dominateth our world!
Sadness is my lot, O Bab Ftuh; wear mourning, O Bab Lgissa,
Shame on you, O place of prayer, the Christian hath defil'd thee!
Even Mulay Amdayl refuses his habitual protection.
Am but a troubadour, and a troubadour wieldeth little power!
I journey like a knave with neither horse nor knapsack,
Laziness doth delay me when I set my foot to the slope!
One night, did dream that I was horse-racing, O Lord,
While around my ears flew bullets from modern rifles!

Though didactic, questionable is the troubadour's role;
Brave is he who can laugh in the face of bullets; on reaching
The plain, the flock stayeth put, though doth complain.
By supporting my spouse have I done a worthy thing,

Yet have witness'd the degradation of our society.
The *jnun* partaketh not of grease but leaveth it in the dish.
Unfortunate be the ugly wife's husband,
Neither beauty nor obedience is hers, the nasty bitch!
Mark my words, O wasteful woman, deceive not thy
Guest, should one perchance appear at thy door!
O Lord, grant unto each human being his share of luck,
May one happiness know, whilst the other liveth in woe!

This traditional ballad of the *tayffart* genre is attributable to the
former *amdyaz* U-Shrif (Ayt Yahya of Tunfit) and was collected
by Arsène Roux, 1932.

An eminently didactic piece, it invokes in its preamble help from
both God and at least two different saints. Somewhat long-winded
and difficult to fathom for the uninitiated, it criticizes stinginess and
the negative role of the traitor, envisaged in local lore as a raven. The
poem also reflects the difficulties that Morocco is going through at
the time of the French conquest (*circa* 1920) – a situation that this
patriotically minded troubadour obviously deplores – as near-
famine and lawlessness stalk the land. The lengthy, apparently
irrelevant, digression on death and interment is actually straight out
of the Sufi tradition. The 'grave exercise', one of the eleven ritual
exercises that enables the believer to achieve *dhikr qalbi*, a state of
well-nigh total communion with God, involves the auto-simulation
of death, a rite not unknown to the Naqshbandi sect of Iraq.

Prophesies of Sidi Bubsher Amhawsh

Blessed be Sidna Muhammad, O Lord,
Guide me along the straight and narrow way!
I am fearful that words will betray me
Should I speak as clearly as the full moon!
I fear naught with thee at my side;
O sword-blows, art no more than wind and rain!
O Christian, great is my wrath; I shall smite
Thy chief, by grace of God and Sidi Ali!
O Sidi Ali u-Brahim, strong be thy hand
Water for to stir, O please, purify me!
Thou art my refuge, O Mulay Abdeslam Wazzani!
Prithee, from my predicament deliver me!
Shouldst thou betray me, O saints, 'tis God's
Pardon that I need, hence my appeal to him!

Speak, O mouth of mine, tell us of new events!
O Lenda, once and future capital that thou art,
The dead alone are entitled to reach thy haven.
How dreadful to hear thee, O raging furnace!
Quoth the asphodel: 'O earthenware pot,
Repudiate me, many have crushed me underfoot!'
Gone is Ahmed U-Haqqar, who lit up the darkness;
O tent-pole, sever'd by steel's inflexible blow!
At Tinteghallin pass did many a hero fall,
Ali Wbawi went down, on whom can we call?
Lo, the master of the tent joyfully welcometh the
Stranger; then cometh the butcher, our ewes to take!
Now gone for ever are our finest givers of milk!
O distress! He hath left us naught but orphan'd lambs!
O enlightened one, tell us the cause of our woe,
Buri'd are our wise men, accursed is our line!

Speak, O mouth of mine, tell us of new events!
O Lqbab, grievous be thy sufferings this year,
Since the Master of the White Towers hath come!
Towards Taqeddust I did wend my way, my thirst
For to quench, yet a giant bird from high in the sky,
Earthwards did plummet and shatter'd my skull!
Am I to laugh, or my distress tearfully vent?
O maiden, thy weeping doth echo from the walls!
Now, how shalt thou dress Ahmari's wound,
Unless thou hast gone, a pitcher of water to fetch.
On my way a hawker did I meet, walking like an Unbeliever;
On my way a tanner I did meet, his disgraceful
Speech put me in mind of our unspeakable Abu Zayd!

O ye possessors of mansions fine and exquisite wall-tiles,
Whilst building is in progress, do exchange courtesies!
Could I but a brazier be, I'd turn from gold to yellow!
My mind in a whirl, I suddenly find myself
Like a nomadic encampment of tents depriv'd;
Without shelter till dawn they squabbl'd!
My mind in a whirl, did I suddenly find myself
Acting demented, ready to repudiate my children's mother,
To wed a harridan, whose belly no offspring provid, eth!
My mind in a whirl, did I suddenly find myself like
The simpleton who prepareth to winnow grain in a
Ravine, of wind's slightest breath devoid!
The Muslim doth to a wild boar liken himself –
Fool, to grub around your snout is ill-equipp'd!

O chiefs, ye that command valiant Ichqern cavalry,
Be not the Ayt Sokhman mere jackal's offspring?
My burden have I shoulder'd, saying: 'With acorns
Shall make shift, of death by hunger I am not afeard!'

My knapsack on my shoulder, all day have I pick'd
Acorns, then homeward do bring this frugal fare,
Only to face complaints from the mistress of the tent!
O Muslims, from firm trigger-fingers cometh salvation,
Didst ever see trigger on musket pulled with little finger?
On the fatal field, till dusk I am surrounded by the fog of battle,
The Senegalese strike more strongly, 'tis the climax!
Till the end, honourably do we acquit ourselves!
O master of the great guns, why should I sire daughters?
Many a chicken have we brought to placate Berger.
Thy pardon I implore, O generous ones whom we saw not!

Here is a ballad of the *tayffart* genre, collected in Lqbab, *circa* 1932, for Arsène Roux by Mulay Hmad, from an Ichqern cobbler named Ali n-Heddu Wssana, who presented it under the above title. As with other *tiyffrin*, the poem features a 'chain' of couplets, each containing two lines (*tiwan*), though an occasional tercet may occur; this kind of lop-sided verse is known as *tamalayt*.

This poem seems something of a 'dog's breakfast', containing as it does, after the usual appeal to God, the Prophet and a miscellany of local saints, a complaint about the French invasion interspersed with parables and traditional couplets, some of them of an apocalyptic nature, attributed to an Imhiwash saint named Sidi Ali Hssayn (1670–1730). Lenda, site of Sultan Mulay Sliman's resounding defeat at the hands of Bubsher Amhawsh (1819), is the mystical heart of the Middle Atlas, where one day the first shall be last, and the last shall be first! A descendant of Bubsher actually still resides there; I had tea with him three or four years back.

Of the many references in the poem, the 'Master of the White Towers' refers to Muha u-Hemmu Zayani, who fought a kind of seven years' war at the turn of the twentieth century against the Ichqern tribe and Sidi Ali Amhawsh; winnowing in a windless spot merely makes the task more arduous; the Ayt Sokhman are a large tribe to the south, on whose territory the Ichqern were not always welcome as evacuees during the 1920s. Taqeddust is the site of a well-known spring near Lqbab; in fact a *café* in that small town bears that very name to this day. Regarding acorns, instances were reported during the Atlas campaigns of starved Berbers grinding these into flour and using them in a rough and ready broth. 'Bershi' was Captain Berger, of the Native Affairs department, often mentioned as both a dour adversary and a benevolent administrator in Berber poetry. His apparent partiality for chicken was common knowledge among the tribesmen who usually contrived to bring some fowl to ingratiate themselves with him. Interestingly, the closing formula, intended to bring the audience back from the poetic dimension to the real world, is of a kind usually found in folk-tales.

Prophesies of Sidi Ali Amhawsh

Wouldst thou witness splendour? Then repair to Lenda;
There will you find minarets that do surpass those in Fez!
Under his rule shall religion prevail, iniquity be banish'd,
Rejoice, O poor wretch, behold the light that shineth!
Riding his horse Sidi Ali shall come and reign over you;
O Berbers, love it or loathe it, I shall your monarch be!
God will strengthen my line, o'er this land shall I reign,
Verily did God promise me that my time would come!
O Berbers, when o'er my yellow face locks hang down,
Then shall come the time for you to lay waste the plain!

Raging from the heights of Atlas, by strong breezes fanned,
The blazing fire hath the people of the Atlantic Plain ravag'd!

Fear spreading, like wild-fire, hath filled town-dwellers' hearts,
O jackal of the high mountains, devour the sheep of the Gharb!
I journeyed to Sefru and Zerhun, like a jackal did howl,
Yet found of Arabs nary a trace – only highland Berbers!
Thou who calleth on Zerhun, cradle of the Idrissiyin!
Fear not; he shall protect thee, to thy side shall hasten!
With his standards the Christian hath our country invaded,
With combative Jews in his midst, he bringeth nought but hatred!
When he doth reach Tinteghallin and Lenda, sad shall be the
Day for the descendants of Sidi Ali Amhawsh!

God alone decideth in what manner the tribes shall unite!
O Berber tribesmen, instructions shall ye receive when the
Christian doth reach Idikel; in that place must ye gather!
Having seen signal fires on Jbal Tujjit, at once did we know
That for Sidi Ali's daughters it foretold days of woe!
May come true Dadda Ali's prophesy about the Rumi.
From corpses of men and horses let pestilential stench arise!
Weary be the jackal, watcheth the fleeing greyhound,
Yet into the hills doth allow his prey to escape!
Come, jackals from Wanargi and Jbal Muriq, do ye
To Tafza repair; go see the furnace that rageth there!
One day on this earth will come men well vers'd in war,
Dismal days shall dawn, O Berbers, with thy drums shall part!

'Seven thousand men and seven thousand horses lay dead,
O Baht, on thy ground!' Thus spake our forefathers!
From Baht one day shall emerge a shaggy black donkey;
To the world his lethal kicks shall turmoil bring!
Nor shall Mount Tget to similar donkey give birth,
It is but where dogs and jackals tear each other to pieces.
From Ayt Myill a great bull did come, pass'd Tafessasset;
Igelgu did reach; thither went a calf from Alemsid.

The bull struck him a fell blow that scatter'd his entrails
On the ground; pittance for pecking chicks did he provide!

When the roses flower in Arekla, southwards shall ye go;
The Ayt Yazem towards the heights will make their way!
Aguray did bring draught animals and seeds to sow, Ayn Luh
Ploughed the furrow; Azru suggested a partnership!
Release water pent up that it may with current flow,
O Sheikh Muhammad, O thou great Bu Khengi!
People truthfully claim that with his maker he made peace,
Worthy of merit was his death, which during a vendetta did occur!
Glory to the Lord, see now what he hath accomplished!
I existed not, then was born, and no longer shall be!
Observe this earth; 'fore God, methinks Sidi Bubsher
Liveth no more; to the encampment he hath not return'd!

Though the original resembled a *tayffart* ('chain') of loose-knit couplets,
the material here is presented as a ballad known as *ahellel* in Azru area,
though there is no conclusive evidence of its constituting one continuous
poem. It is largely based on a version collected by Hussa u-Muha from
Assu u-Seyd Lemtiri in May 1966. The actual authenticity of the lines is
debatable, the material having passed through numerous retellings and
re-workings. Many other versions exist, with fragments surfacing here and
there, right across the Fazaz region, even in recent years.

Again, this poem combines pronominal ambiguity with not a little
opacity. Variously attributed to Sidi Ali Amhawsh (1860–1918)
and/or to his great-grandfather Sidi Bubhser Amhawsh (late
eighteenth to early nineteenth centuries), it consists of a catalogue
of utterances, reputedly prophetic and often apocalyptic in nature,
the subject matter of which may be somewhat off-putting, though
the careful reader will have noted a reference to the battle of Baht
(cf. the first verse in this anthology). By and large, these prophesies
represent the stock-in-trade of the Imhiwash line of saints,

endowed with soothsaying and diverse other magical powers, thanks to which they exercise considerable influence over the Middle Atlas tribes. As a result they worked hard to unite the latter in their resistance to central government in the eighteenth and nineteenth centuries, and against the French until 1932, making use of a supposed Arab/Berber dichotomy (actually a kind of Highland versus Lowland separation), of which there is some evidence in this poem. Indeed, Sidi Bubsher and his descendants were perceived as a potential dynastic threat, as they clearly had plans combining the spiritual and the temporal, including a problematic Idrissid restoration (observe the allusion to Zarhun, with which the Idrissid are linked), and centred on Lenda as a possible future capital, as may be gathered from some of the above stanzas. This partly explains why the Alawi sultanate left no stone unturned in its efforts to curb their power. References to Ayt Myill, Idikel, Tujjit, Tafessaset and Tafza (near Tazizawt), recall various milestones of resistance to the French advance. Otherwise a jumble of ideas, with, in one of the more obscure passages, apocalyptic allusions to a black donkey reminding one of the *dujjal* tradition, surrounding a nebulous, donkey-riding variety of Anti-Christ, forerunner of the true Mahdi, that is prevalent in these parts. Parabolic references to dogs, jackals, greyhounds and other animals recall various battles in the Middle Atlas both in pre-colonial and colonial times.

Ballad on Tazizawt

O Prophet, O father of Fadma, sweet thy name when
Utter'd in honourable discourse, O Sidna Muhammad!
O Sidna Bubsher, of Lenda the glorious victor,
Thy protection I crave as through the land I roam!
As I set out on the way, prudence he doth urge;
Placing one foot before 'tother, the abyss is never far!
O father of Fadma, O my Lord Muhammad the Arab,
And ye too, O Sidi Driss and Sidi Lahbib!
O sheikh, go, escort the approaching caravan,
O bride's father, and thou too, Sidi Muhand,
Leave me not defenceless; watch over me!
O Sidi Bennasr let the saint of the mountains stay
Close and protect me. Be he merciful to me, together
With Sidi Bu Muhand and of Aruggu the master!

Of mere words my discourse – nothing written!
Be they bless'd, O Lord in whom I put my trust!
Repeat, O my mouth, what hath come to pass,
Since, unshackled by God, across this land I roam!
Never hath my impetuous heart favoured me,
Can no longer control it, strength hath deserted me!
Deceitful clerics have betrayed us, driven me distraught,
Such fork'd tongues, how could I in saints put my trust?
I shall from the Ayt Hediddu beg my broth. If wisdom do
Retain, after this shall ne'er again in *igurramn* believe!
O Lord, contemplate the darkness that reigneth over Islam,
Such humiliation vile, such chastisement on us inflicted!
O sons of the Prophet, vanquish'd we be by the enemy,
In the wake of Amharoq's fail'd embassy!

The *igurramn* did say: 'Tazizawt was for the final stand
Place appointed!' Hiding in caverns was the mujahideen's
Undoing; hunger more lethal than bullets vanquish'd famish'd
Fighters! Didst help each other, O sons of Tujjit? Starving
People behave – 'tis a fact – like a herd put out to graze!
O ye that did saintly leaders follow, didst thou not see?
For Tazizawt defenders were unable bread to provide!
'Twas not juniper broth that prov'd irksome; 'twas by
Guns that the sons of Tujjit were crush'd; heaven help us!
O demented ones how can I be reconcil'd with our leader,
By his decision do we with the Rumi blindly consort!
The order to capitulate from Heaven did come, else how
Could we continue? Now the Rumi doth dictate his terms!

May thy pardon, O Lord, be extended to the mujahideen;
Unpunish'd, they commit robbery and other misdemeanour!
Do betray and cut each others' throats, 'midst the hills the
Strong bullies the weak! Our saints did announce the Rumi's
Defeat; when rose their prayers, aeroplanes did appear!
We prayed the planes might fall, or be by guns destroy'd, until
Disaster struck, O Ayt Tazizawt, hidden in holes and caverns!
Lord, the caves in which you hid, your graves did become!
So many good men died to serve as mere carrion for jackals!
When all is said and done, hunger prov'd of mujahideen the ruin;
Didst e'er such weeping hear among orphans and widows?
Letting his hair grow, the bard towards the hated foe did go;
O Prophet, O father of Fadma, sweet is thy name!

A ballad of the *tamdyazt* genre on the Tazizawt battle, collected for
Arsène Roux by a certain Muhammad Ben Askri from an anonymous Ayt
Sokhman bard in 1933.

This is a good example of the way Berber bards treat a topic such as this battle, which took place in 1932. After invoking God, his Prophet and various saints, rather than giving a blow-by-blow account, the poem makes allusions and draws conclusions from mistakes committed. Though reference is made to *igurramn* and to 'our leader', not once is Sidi Lmekki mentioned by name; his brothers even less so. The last of the Amhawsh line, he chose to make his stand against the French on Tazizawt in the summer of 1932, as a result of posthumous instructions left by his father Sidi Ali Amhawsh. Believing in his prophesies of imminent French defeat, the Berber fighters remained confident and defiant till the last. Embassies sent some days before the battle by the Zayan chief Amharoq, urging the mujahideen to surrender, had failed. Many of the resistance fighters, referred to in the poem as 'Ayt Tazizawt' or 'Ayt Tujjit', had previously been on nearby Jbal Tujjit, dug in deep to escape the effects of artillery fire and eventually died on the spot, less from bombs and bullets than sheer hunger. Daily fare was poor indeed: juniper-flavoured broth, locusts, even grass, and acorns ground into flour, a disappointing substitute for bread; it had been too early to harvest their wheat-fields when the Berber irreconcilables and their families had set up camp on Tazizawt in early summer. During the final days of the month-long siege, when French-led troops took out the dissident foxholes and rifle-pits one by one, there was some unruliness and in-fighting in the ranks of the resistance. Eventually, those who refused to surrender broke out through the encircling French forces and sought refuge in Ayt Hediddu country where the resistance flag was still flying. There was a lot of bitterness over Sidi Lmekki's capitulation, even more when he was appointed *qayd* over the Ayt Sokhman a couple of years later.

Short poems on Tazizawt

Thus spake Tawjjaaout hill: 'Had it not been for those Zayan,
Never would dogs in hob-nailed boots have scal'd my heights!'

Tawjjaaout repeated: 'In our shelter a candle did light,
But no fire kindl'd lest even greater disaster befall!'

Thus spoke Bu Genfu hill: 'When I felt those hob-nail'd
Boots, did know that to the enemy they belong'd!'

Could I but thrust Sidi Lmekki's head into a boxwood thicket,
Would make him smell camel carcasses to remind him of all
Those wretches who did vainly camp with him in the hills!

By Sidi Lmekki's false words was I deceiv'd; now that the
Muslims have surender'd, no doubt he will be appointed *qayd*!

Prophesies of the Ayt Sidi Ali prov'd to be falsehood;
Henceforth I can but trust in the French officer's word!

Is dismay'd he who, passing at Tazizawt, the mujahideen's
Encampment doth descry. Bleach'd bones of man and
Beast on the soil lie intermingl'd!

Long wilt thou remain in my mind, O Tazizawt, as a war
In which with rifle-fire the Rumi did destroy the Prophet!
Brothers Lmehdi and Lmurtada were like unto little
Lambs that die in the enclosure from a surfeit of thyme!
Forgive He that separateth plough'd land from fallow,
Who created sun and stars; the whole world doth grieve,
O thou who promis'd forgiveness if the oath we swore!
To Tazra did make my way and reach'd it feeling footsore,
A cave I there did dig, enter'd it and slept for evermore!

A brief medley of *tamawayt*-style verse mostly attributed to local poetess Tawkhettalt.

Tawjjaout hill was a strategic position, the scene of a desperate battle between mujahideen and Zayan warriors fighting on the French side; its capture threw open the whole resistance defensive system on its south side. Bu Genfu was the hill up which the French, 'the dogs wearing hob-nailed boots' (*igdi bu yferghusn*), dragged their heavy guns to subject Tazizawt to a round-the-clock bombardment. Sidi Muhand Lmehdi and Sidi Lmurtada were two firebrand brothers of Sidi Lmekki's, whose conduct was exemplary – both died hero's deaths before the end of the siege. In their foxholes and bunkers resistance fighters had to avoid lighting fires at night for fear of being machine-gunned. For many of them, these holes ultimately became their graves. As for bones, some were still tragically visible in the Ashlu ravine in 2007.

Ballad against Sidi Lmekki

Thus spoke Sidi Lmekki: 'By God's grace, let us feast and rejoice,
I did dream that of the *ayt bujjur* they had appointed me *qayd*!'
Said Sidi Lmekki: 'Shall capture those sons of dogs and make
Playthings of them!' But 'twas his sons that the Christian did capture!
Quoth Sidi Lmekki: 'A silver bullet did my father bequeath me!'
But Ayt Hediddu fighters knew that those were but vain words!
Said Sidi Ali: 'Sidi Lmekki's misdeeds I care not to contemplate;
As for your homes, consum'd they be like straw in the furnace!'
Dew-drenched grass affects but sheep taken out early to pasture;
Woe is me, the saint I follow'd in midday heat on burning slopes!
Your thunder can ne'er forget, O Tazizawt; inside me still echoes!
The chance visitor to Ashlu will not contradict you, O U-Sokhman!

Planes daily bombard me, famine torments me, shells
Shatter rocks above my head, causing havoc amidst my
Herds of sheep, camel and cattle as they cross the pass!
To Anergi I did go, also to Hamdun and U-Lghazi; after reaching
Tanut n-Bu Wurgher, my steps did retrace; became a mere muleteer!
By God I do swear: I shall neither shave nor bathe on feast-days;
Do now bid goodbye to adventures distant and hopes vain!
Behold, O Lord, without malice or after-thought I did surrender,
O Justice Divine, spare me of burning faggots the punishment!
His belly full of beans Alibush the traitor has the Prophet forsaken.
Would that I never have to cross in his company the fatal plank!
Woe betide that interpreter, the French captain and Alibush, too,
Since society has been level'd – serfs and lords no more!

Dignity notwithstanding, under the French orders are to be obey'd.
A man I remain yet outside the captain's office, I become an orphan!
When the guard strikes me, I must be respectful; call him 'My Lord!'
Whereas the knave has little of a lord! 'All this', said Sidi Lmekki,
'Is by God decreed; 'twas not my decision that we should surrender!'
Could I but a traveller find, would rally fighters in the hills still
Resisting, tell them: 'Eat frugal food, never cave in to those cowards!'
By the Almighty, for tomorrow do aspire to Grace Divine; as for
Worldly food, 'tis as with spinning: easy one day, irksome the next!
About Sidi Lmekki harsh words have people pronounc'd, yet he
Did try his best! God willing let him show mercy to our heroes,
May the good shepherd accompany us, that we form one flock!

This is a well-known ballad of the *tayffart* genre, highly critical role of Sidi
Lmekki's role in the Tazizawt battle. The author is unknown, though the
poem is now generally attributed to poetess Tawkhettalt. The present
text was assembled from various fragments, the chronology of the
material having been somewhat re-worked by me.

The poet, joined by Sidi Ali Amhawsh speaking from the grave, castigates Sidi Lmekki, whom he has blindly followed, sharing in the discomfort and danger of Tazizawt, vainly hoping for delivery when the marabout fires his silver bullet! A shell-shocked survivor, he recalls the horror of the battle, the final stand above Tazra in rugged Ashlu ravine with its boxwood bushes and stunted evergreen oak. After the surrender, he wanders from place to place till he grudgingly accepts the job of muleteer, or animal-driver (asewwagi), a low-ranking occupation to which these poets often refer as an alternative to working for the Christian. Yet, ultimately, bow down he must to his new masters – the French *qebtan*, Alibush the traitor and a guard who undeservedly insists on being called 'My Lord' and regularly beats him. Deeply discouraged to the point of regretting his surrender to the French (literally those 'Jews wearing *képis*'), he places the blame fairly and squarely on Sidi Lmekki, now exposed as a conman rather than a worthy leader, though there remains a hint of ambiguity surrounding his role in the last lines.

Ballad of Ayt Ndhir

Thy name I invoke, O fertiliser of seed 'neath the earth,
That doth ensure harvest rich on arid ground!
Lord, 'tis thy name that the ploughman first pronounceth,
When he soweth seed, in thee his trust doth place!
On barren, unirrigated soil the seed doth sow;
But Almighty God is of plentiful waters the provider!
In profusion moisture-laden clouds the Lord shall send,
Generous rain shall penetrate the earth deeply!
Let us now come to the purpose of our discourse,
Like the horseman who tighteneth rein to change course.

In these hard times to the Rumi goes God's preference;
In the sky he is supreme with planes, on earth with tanks!
He has seal'd a pact with *jnun*; when something comes to
Pass, by telegraph the officer is at once appris'd.
Yesteryear a month's walk was necessary to reach the coast
From Tunfit; now in a minute is sent the word!
The Christian a transmitter doth possess, with mailbags
From telegraphs poles suspended; of a secretary no need!
Contingents of Senegalese did muster, together with *Joyeux*,
Droves of Muslims, too; the Christian order'd them forward!
Great be thy prowess, O mujahid, yet the times are a-changing!
From earth to high heaven, the Christian can but victorious be!

Whether you flee or remain, your ploughing neglect not,
Be sure, in all things, to honour our forefathers' traditions!
What hath befallen Sidi Rehhu, and his Ayt Ndhir allies?
The one and the other like diminutive insects crush'd!
In the van of the Christian forces, march Zayan and Marakkech
Contingents, with them Ayt Izdeg and Ayt Myill tribesmen!
Like birds of prey his planes o'er the wooded hills do hover;
Like craven chickens the mujahideen take to flight!
Trenches ye may dig, or palisades erect, yet naught will avail;
Wherever ye lurk, from heaven on high he shall strike!
Lenda he did take; though Tazizawt had for the Christian
Hot reception prepar'd, in the hills was Islam vanquish'd!

Senegalese and *Joyeux* their evil business do accomplish;
Quarter neither requested nor given – red is the ground with gore!
Poorly do the combatants compare; the soldier with waterbottle
And bread-loaf; the mujahid with torn sandals and oatmeal cakes!
In battle, cunning avails but little, 'tis more a matter of destiny;
Strive as you may, if your time is come, death shall claim you!
Regain your castles, O Ayt Hediddu, your defeat was written;

Before you we took up arms, now the officer is our *hakem*!
How many of ours did say: 'The spade I shall never wield!'
See the proud ones today as about their lawful business they go!
Thy name I pronounce, thou that dost to fish life impart,
E'en raiment warm, that they may in water survive!

This ballad of the *tayffart* genre is taken from the repertoire of the U-Ndhir bard, Seyd u-Brahim and was collected by Arsène Roux in Azru, March 1933.

The Tazizawt bastion has fallen, but the Ayt Hediddu and a handful of other southeast Moroccan tribes have yet to be conquered. But the poet makes no bones about the fact that further resistance is futile, given the staggering military superiority of the French, coupled with their almost magical powers, highlighted by such inventions as the telegraph, the aeroplane and the tank. It is also quite plain from this account that the French make extensive use of native auxiliaries as cannon fodder, sending them out in front to catch the first bullets. The poet, himself of the Ayt Ndhir tribe, explains how earlier resistance to the conqueror quickly collapsed and a French Native Affairs Officer, known colloquially as the *hakem*, or *qebtan*, substituted a cut-and-dried, Cartesian style of everyday administration for the earlier customary law based on collective oath-swearing.

Poetic fragments on the Atlas endgame

Being a bachelor I am happy my marching orders to
Receive; Jbal Qusr my destination; thither must I go!

When the Christian our uniforms did distribute, I realised
That soon a-soldiering we would go; but had hoped till then
That he would send us back to our tents.

Should I perchance with the French a-soldiering go
I will to my utmost the Prophet's laws respect!

Long have I travell'd the highways and by-ways,
O Muslims, from whence shall come our salvation?

Slap my face and pluck my beard, O Christian,
To your monarch has our king sold us!

In the plain the Christian has his outpost set up; go join
Him if you are not afeard of a prison sentence!

If a bomb explodes in the plain, our cavaliers flee
Like sheep when the jackal attacks the herd!

Haunted by the owl's mocking call and nigh to death,
You are this day defenceless, O El-Herri battlefield!

Aghbala weeps enough to drive Ikusal to tears,
Bu Wattas does likewise; what of you, O Tizi n-Tawrirt?

What sad times! Neither Lhajj Waaskri nor
Hamman n-Ayt Waqqa can do aught to save me;
Go fight the enemy, 'tis the only way out!

What sad times! I can do aught but weep bitterly,
Since even Jews now saddle up and ride horses!

Diverse and many are the Christian's armies,
To confront them we can but count on ourselves!

Rotten and worthless be the world,
On all sides by aeroplanes beset!

High in the heavens planes fly overhead,
Methinks they're the horsemen of the apocalypse,
Truly, the end is in sight!

High in the heavens planes fly overhead,
Tell me, O Lord, what can I do?

High in the heavens planes fly overhead,
I call'd my brother, but nary a reply did come;
Then I knew that he was no more!

Ceaselessly they do strike the earth; O planes,
We are exhausted! Your fire devastates the land!

O master of planes, since my surrender, on me do
Blows rain down; could I but join Sidi Ali and his fighters,
Then the blows would rain down on you!

Where are the Prophet and the Ayt Sidi Ali?
Gone is Islam; you walk no more in God's ways,
O people, you fear him not!

Gone is Islam, of war a casualty!
O laws of Sidi Muhand, I respect ye no longer!

Everybody speaks of *jihad* on this the day of God's
Discomfiture; yet, the Christian has won – 'tis a fact!

To declare his religion the Prophet to Tujjit did go;
The saints also went there, solemn conclave to hold!

Did roam o'er hill and dale; found none but cowards!
O Muslims, from whence shall come our salvation?

By day and by night do aught but fight;
Salvation can but come from use of the rifle!

If God could but help me find the Rumi,
Surely, to burn him would I light a wood fire!

Would that I could go and steal a Chassepot rifle,
Dig in at the pass, and hold out to the bitter end!

Should I thus anguish in jail? 'Twould be better
By far to join the mountaineers and defy authority!

Fadma, my dear, beware of the Jew! Trust not the
Christian who shall come after; choose but a
Fighter most brave, who wields well the bayonet!

Could I but find the enchanted land wherein
Shall in concord live Jew and Muslim!

Pray tell me, O Lord, was Buazza's body recovered
By his horsemen, or did the dissidents make off with it?

O horsemen, what prompted you to charge near Alemsid?
Now Buazza is dead; cold the steel that pierced his entrails!

O Tunfit! The despicable Senegalese camp in the surrounding
Hills; and are now by telegraph linked to the Christians!

O frog-eater, sure of yourself as you are, just follow Asif Udghas
To Tunfit; there shall the villagers give you a good thrashing!

Thus spoke Bab n-Uyyad hill: 'O Juniper Pass,
The Rumi draws near; comes the time to smite him!'

O man from Ayt Yahya, your homeland calls you;
Do come and irrigate your fields of maize!

Smite with all thy might, O man from Ayt Hediddu!
'Twill nothing change; like me shall you bondage know!

Could I but mud smear on my cheeks
Or be carried away into the Hereafter,
Now that cowards rule in the land of heroes!

Short snatches of Ichqiren and Ayt Myill poetry, mostly of the
tamawayt genre, together with a few *izlan*, collected by Arsène
Roux in 1934 from Ba-Ahssin ould Dadda Ali of Khenifra;
translated in Ifrane by me in the spring of 2001, with help from
Labha Elasri and Lahssen Lmejdub.

This ensemble gives a true-to-life portrayal of the frame of mind
most Berbers experienced during the closing chapter of the con-
quest, whether in the ranks of the resistance, among those recently
submitted to the French, or serving with the latter as Goumiers or
mokhaznis in the final 1933 operations in Jbal Qusr and Hediddu-
land. Two couplets refer to the fate of the dashing cavalier, Buazza,
one of Muha u-Hemmu's sons, fighting on the French side. Again,
the universal sense of shame is vividly rendered, especially in the
wake of the surrender of the discredited Ayt Sidi Ali at Tazizawt in
1932, as is the parlous state of the Muslim faith, shattered by so
many disasters. The fact that even Jews, up till then reduced
practically to non-person status in feudal Morocco, are raising their
heads, is indicative of changing times. However, lost in the flood of
complaint, defiance and indignation is a little couplet in which the
poet longs for an ideal land where Jew and Muslim could be
friends, actually reflecting one of the preoccupations among
today's Moroccan Imazighen.

Ballad on Second World War

O envoy of God, O mighty intercessor, O Prophet, in thee we
Trust, sweet sounding is thy name; Satan get thee hence!
Speak of other things we must, oppressive be the heat;
Without thee, O one and only God, I am feeble and helpless!
The French have indeed defeated us, yet grateful and admiring
Are we; widows and orphans every spring do grain receive!
Their officers are good to us; have by decree our customs agreed
To preserve, fasting and prayer to the Prophet are respected!
Though they be our victors, they are not without merit; vendettas are
Banned, arms set aside, enemies now partake of the same dish!

Under Marshall Lyautey's rule, life was like butter, as
Beautiful as a bed of roses, 'twas indeed a happy time!
Sugar and soap to be had in abundance, likewise tea,
Cotton, and goods aplenty unladen from merchant ships!
Successive waves of sweating, richly caparisoned horses
Would, on each feast day, thunder past in powder-play!
When Pétain commanded, to Noguès did he entrust Muslims'
Welfare, saying: 'Vanquished them we did, but ours they now are!'
'Forget not!' added he, 'some with settlers toil, some serve in the
Goums, yet others contribute as guards to maintain law and order!'

'Morocco's destiny lies in thy hands. 'Twas with the Sultan's
Sanction, lest we forget, that we pacified the various regions!'
Cleverly have the French preserved peace in our land; wise
Is their rule with customary law tribunals and appeal courts!
'Twas for Morocco like a fine spring of pastures green,
Till war did come to blight the very roots of this fertility!
Then the Americans came, pastmasters in heavy industry.
Overabundant their production: cars, tanks, ships and planes.

Tractors arrived, together with implements of all sorts,
Providing all the necessary, to them like child play.
In five days they can assemble a wagon, build a brick wall;
Fire do possess that can desiccate water, or burn weeds.

As for Germans and Italians, leave them to their sad fate, O Lord,
Evil people that they be! Horrible their deeds, keep them far away!
Stealthily with planes did come, bombarded a few miserable huts,
Then untruthfully claimed to have devastated Casablanca!
Sooth to say, only by paupers was Derb Sultan inhabited, yet,
As thieves in the night they struck, empty-handed flew away!

This traditional ballad of the *tayffart* genre had a command performance
by Middle Atlas bard Seyd u-Brahim Lmtiri, broadcast on Radio Maroc
some time in 1943–4. It was recopied and retranslated by Arsène Roux
in Bayonne in 1965.

An edifying piece of wartime, pro-Allied propaganda, it speaks
in glowing terms of Marshall Lyautey's proconsulship, of the
pacification of Morocco by the French army in the sultan's name and
of the contribution by numerous locals to policing the country in
the ranks of the Goum and *mokhazni* units. Interestingly, a positive
picture is given of the arrangements of the so-called 'Berber *dahir*',
with its insistence on customary law (*izerf*), which was highly
criticised at the time by the Salafi-inspired Nationalist elements in
Morocco. This is, all in all, a very Manichean piece, the French and
Americans being presented in a favourable light, while their Axis
opponents are vilified.

Ballad about the Nationalists

Let us to the Prophet pray, O distributor of bounty,
Verily there is none other to match thee, O Lord!
Master of the waves, master of destiny, master of choice,
Hold hell at arm's length, O master of the oceans!
Master of the moon and stars, thy protection we crave!
Come, O my tongue, tell me what hath come to pass!
The one and true God ceaselessly doth watch,
In these troubled times, troubled be the waters, too!
Bitter the waters that the Imhiwash saints did mention,
Life Here Below is in the grip of unwonted turmoil!

On your guard must you remain in others' company,
Report not what you hear lest events untoward befall!
Pray that the down-and-out will hold his tongue;
Should you see two persons together, keep away;
Act the fool and say: 'I have but recently arrived!'
Lest trouble cause you, e'en of your coat beware!
Hurt shall come from he whom you hold dear;
Observe the stranger from afar, 'twill be all right!
In the crowd, other people their ears open wide.
Help no more your neighbour lest misfortune follow!
From the Nationalists no escape – e'en by hiding at home;
Careful whom you meet – 'tis easy to end up in trouble!

In these times, each man seeks his neighbour to destroy;
Accusations easily made: 'He works for the government!'
From lbiru you must stay away, three months, nay twelve.
Villagers' sad plight can be but the local councillor's fault,
Who has their votes purchased and taken his role too lightly!
Put not your trust in elected councillors, at lbiru are for

Oppression responsible; the land has from earthquake recovered,
O civil servant, evictions have, like lightning poor people struck!
Like the cat of the Ayt Tulal, injustice be your motto,
Of dunning your hapless parishioners you think nothing!
When victims accuse you of partiality, O swindler,
'I alone am entitled to speak!' is your sole reply!

Those who did money give are the ones who signed,
The swindler has but paid them back the price of meat eaten.
The Nationalists have on the *hakem* inflicted grievous hurt,
As cruel as a panther's bite! Now angrily he sits in his office!
Each Nationalist who appears before him is handed
First a spade then, without further ado, a pickaxe!
The Nationalists are like the rogue elephant who, not content to
Despoil tribes by day, sends his mate to ravage their fields by night!
He who reaches *lbiru* is like the sheep fleeced by a thorn-tree,
Whatever the outcome, he is fated to lose his fleece!
The true Believer keeps his own council, speaks to no man;
Should somebody call out to him, turns a deaf ear!
Let him further hold his peace; by staying away from *lbiru*,
He who believes in God, shall stay out of trouble!

A ballad of the *tayffart* genre by Seyd u-Brahim Lmtiri on Nationalist
activities during the run-up to independence. It was collected for
Arsène Roux by Hamani u-Milud in December 1953 and translated by
me in November 2007, with help from Haddou Khettouch.

While openly critical of the Nationalists, the poet also denounces
abuses of power by civil servants. The poem portrays the atmo-
sphere of suspicion that prevails in the land, with subversive
activities poisoning the atmosphere and careless talk potentially
landing all and sundry in trouble, the situation made more
complex by corrupt Moroccan councillors more concerned with

self-enrichment than furthering the interests of their charges. This situation does little to enhance the authorities' reputation, while those suspected of Nationalist activities are punished by hard labour Hence, to avoid complications, it is preferable not to frequent *lbiru* where the disgruntled *hakem* sits, convinced that he had done his job conscientiously and angry at his diminishing prestige.

Ode to Zayd u-Hmad

With thy name I do commence, O Lord!
There is none greater than thee, O Almighty!
Thou hast the sun, moon and stars created
To light the traveller's way, by night and day!
I am a mere bard who seeketh inspiration,
That my words may fall upon the right ears,
That they may from the audience attention draw,
That e'en the deaf may know the truth!

'Tis not for a maiden fair that grieves my heart,
Surely not for a sumptuous beauty, that I sing!
Nor for you, mother and father, O parents dear,
But for a man whose fame spans earth and sky,
For fraternity's sake and fellowship friendly!
'Tis of a panther that I sing, Zayd u-Hmad was
His name, who spurned imprisonment by the
Rumi, whose injustice he utterly rejected!
Over him the moon and stars did watch as he crossed
The plains, climbed cliffs, or endured midday heat!
He left his wife and progeny, leading a life of thrift,
Egged on by resentment, both the drum and plough
Did forsake, in his eyes shone the light of battle,
Concern'd as he was by his kinsfolk's plight!

Heedless of hunger and thirst, fearlessly he took to the
Mountain wastes and many a European slayed!
Long and well, of that impious blood the parched
Earth drank its fill, till its thirst had quenched!
He forsook woollen carpets and home comforts,
Rocky earth his bed, a stone pillow for his head!
Making light of harsh conditions, cold and heat,
Even of fierce lions, whose company he sought.
Deadly cobras shunned him, as he the Rumi defied,
A lean, sinewy athlete, equal to every occasion,
His hawk-like eye from a distance his adversary
Detected, before striking him lightning-like;
His quick brain and agility gifts by God granted!

A thorn in the Rumi's flesh he did become, hindering
The enemy's movements; counter-measures of no avail!
Bearing a charmed life, he outwitted him at every turn,
Quite vainly did the Rumi attempt to bring him to book.
But can the panther to the jackal contemplate surrender?
Against him the timorous Rumi was ever powerless.
Pray, does the desert lizard with the serpent consort?
Or highflying eagle with earthbound huntsman meet?
The Rumi knows not Zayd u-Hamd, the Amazigh
Warrior, nor the paths he follows – but Zayd knows his!
Verily was Zayd u-Hmad a noble Amazigh fighter!
Fearful of treason, in fit of high dudgeon Zayd slew
Some of his companions, though later lived to regret it,
Disrupting households, making of children orphans!

But even should the heavens come to fall,
An avenging weapon ne'er shall leave his hand!
Zayd has donned the turban of bravery,
Declaring his honour, becoming e'en greater!

Classic Oral Poetry from the Middle Atlas   81

Then was noised abroad news of your death!
At dawn the sun no longer rose as was its wont,
On the morn of the Aïd you slew him, O Rumi,
Fateful day that shall ever live in infamy!
At Tadafalt was perpetrated the fell deed,
Horrified the villagers to see the great Zayd,
Like a lamb led to slaughter, make of his
Faith in God the sacrifice, for this land of
Our birth, that we might in freedom live!

O Zayd, man of unperishable renown, your
Name is on everybody's lips, great or humble!
Your name lives on in our annals, our traditions,
Even if the iniquitous have of your grave lost trace!
Your name remains hallowed, e'er green the memory!
For the sake of fraternity and fellowship friendly!
Verily was Zayd u-Hmad a noble Amazigh fighter!

A classic ballad of *tamdyazt* genre, author unknown; collected
for me by Lahssen u-Gwelmim at Warzazat in February 1984.

The style and allusions to the 'noble Amazigh fighter' clearly situate
this piece in the period that followed the Berber renaissance of the
early 1980s. Otherwise the reader will observe familiar character-
istics such as pronominal permutation and absence of chronology.
A controversial figure, alternating between mere desperado and
Robin Hood-style hero, Zayd u-Hmad has acquired freedom fighter
status for his one-man campaign against France in the years
following the surrender on Jbel Baddu in summer 1933. Zayd held
out for three years in the barren hills, waylaying French officers,
gunning down Legionnaires and native auxiliaries, even robbing
wealthy Moroccan merchants, until every man's hand was against
him and he was finally betrayed and killed at Tadafalt, near Tinghir,

early in 1936. Note how the legend has grown around his person, especially the 'lion companion', a motif usually associated with Atlas saints rather than freedom fighters.

On life's tribulations

See the misfortune hidden in my heart; should it on
My face appear, 'twould make it as black as a slave's!
O mountain springs, 'tis not water that I thirst after,
I do sorely miss brothers, kinfolk and family!
Could God but turn me into a winged vulture that
Would wheel tirelessly above our encampments!
O spring where abideth my companion, could I but
Pitch my tent there, the better to watch over him!
In the dead of night Love will whisk me away,
Walls or locked doors will be of no avail!
O death, thou art like unto the sheep-trader,
Who selecteth the best animals to slaughter!
O shaking teeth, part we must; what's the
Use, my mouth doth suffer overmuch pain!
May God destroy thee, O undeserved enemy,
May all men witness thy shameful downfall!

This was described to me as a ballad fragment belonging to the *tanshad* genre, and was collected by Fatima Elasri from her mother, Ayn Luh (Ayt Myill), in May 1993.

Hospitality betrayed

To fresh matters must I now refer, indeed there's much to say.
One night I spent as a passing guest in a friend's house.
Sufficient was the meal, even though today, come what may,
Some men are reluctant to open their door to visitors.
It takes but little patience to spend the evening together,
Enough time for intentions, worthy and unworthy, to show.
Say what I must, these times are at once good and bad.
As to what fate holds in store, how should we know?
We lack nothing material, yet our minds are in turmoil!

God be merciful towards us – except for heretics!
Neither by day nor by night have I prayed,
Yet expect that circumstances shall prove favourable!
Stronger than ours the faith of Jews and Christians,
Who keep their word and indulge not in falsehood!
A promise once made is unswervingly respected,
Whereas Muslims are usually untrustworthy liars!
Did you hear what upset the villagers at Turbdid?
Great is their distress since the death of a guest.
Who will now near a house dare unfold his pallet?

Along came a trader from Ayt Merghad heading
For market, as was his wont, supplies to purchase,
Like others, at the sweat of his brow earning a living.
Tightly fasten'd did the U-Merghad his knapsack carry.
His stock-in-trade? Why, a bag of green gravel,
Remedy much in demand from chance purchasers.
He hoped to sell his wares to travelling harvesters.
On market day did he cross Bab n-Wayyad.
Happy was an U-Hediddu to spy the newcomer,
Invited him into his car, so they travell'd together.

On they drove, reached the village of Alemghu. Said the
U-Hediddu: 'Come spend the night at my house!
'Tis now too late customers to find, they are all abed!
Come with me. Tomorrow, early shall you rise'.
Taking him by the cloak, a friendly gesture, he drew him
Forward. Yet towards his grave did entice him!
With a great stone he dealt his guest a fatal blow;
On the ground lay the man, as by a grindstone crushed!
Well, traitor, was it hunger alone that motivated you?
He did divest him of what little wealth he possessed,
But now, what profit will he derive thereof?

Everlasting life shall ever be the lot of the rightful,
Who earn their living at the sweat of their brow.
As for ill-gotten gain, thief's reward shall be pain!
With blindness did God strike the evil U-Hediddu!
For having surmised that his guest was a rich man,
He shall suffer Here Below, aye, and in the Hereafter!
With blindness did God strike the evil U-Hediddu!
Neither rich merchant nor wealthy tourist did he slay;
'Twas but an elderly vendor of stones, for which
Crime he has received well-deserved chastisement!

In peace I do wish to live, trusting in fellow Berbers,
Whereas in big cities, with mixed population, crime is rife,
Women, newborn babes, all are victims of misfortune!
For a handful of coins a man will slay his neighbour!
In these times, e'en the highlands are dangerous,
The rot having spread to Aghbala and Imilshil!
Also at Ayn Leuh, flocks drink from sullied waters!
No safety in sleeping near a nomads' encampment!
With thy name do I commence, O Lord, thou and
Thy eternal dwelling-place!

A well-known contemporary ballad of the *tamdyazt* genre, composed by the famous Sheikh Assu of Ishishawn (Ayt Yahya), more commonly known as Lisiwr. I collected the first version collected in autumn 1983 at Midelt (courtesy of Hmad ou-Chrif from Ayt Hediddu, Imedghas); a second version figures in Khettouch (2007: 50–6).

This is a typically didactic piece denouncing declining moral values, and includes unexpected praise for Jews and Christians. It also features pronominal permutation, a trait by now familiar to the reader, in which the narrator directly comments on the action. The poem relates the untimely demise of a man from Ayt Merghad travelling on business through Ayt Hediddu country. Hospitality being one of the cornerstones of Moroccan society, failure to comply with its sacred obligations is a crime, in this instance made even worse by murder. Bab n-Wayyad, Alemghu and Imilshil are place-names in Hediddu-land; Aghbala is in Ayt Sokhman country; Ayn Leuh a small town in the Middle Atlas.

Old-time amorous and didactic verse

As we pilgrims set forth, guarantee our safety, O Lord,
Both on the way out and when we're homeward bound!

Whose castles do I see yonder, whose lands
Do I roam? For you do I yearn, O my native heath!

Who knows, my native land, whether I shall e'er
Set eyes on you again, or if in some far country,
An unknown pass shall mark my final resting-place!

I beseech you have mercy while I remain here below!
O love, ere I depart this life, now that my time is come,

Thy hospitality I do earnestly crave, O native land,
Ere I set off on the journey to the great unknown!

Itto, her name is ever on my lips as I rise, as I sleep,
As I go forth – even on death's day; I would fain have
This upright girl to keep the home fires burning!

From the wooded hill, from the plain, from the sky
Did love come to me, sent by my sweetheart!

Bow down, O mountain, I beseech you, become a flat
Plain that I may reach my beloved who abides beyond!

How can I cross the mountain to reach my lover? There is
Naught but melting snow that rots the cedars; no way is safe!

I stood there watching the pass, the wind stinging my eyes,
Straining to catch a glimpse of my beloved; yet he came not!

Painfully the stork did climb the pass, crossed the
Peaks; on arriving did strike the platter with her
Beak, but of meat there was none!

I would fain travel down the stony track, be by jackals
Devoured, and torn to pieces by vultures rather than endure
Earthly life with its load of tribulation and woe!

Remember, how thine eyes turned away from me;
Remember, you did withdraw your hand when I touched you;
Remember, you fettered the feet that once bore you to my side;
Remember, how you did break the vow we made;
See how despicable my lover has become!

I am like he who builds an ice-castle by night,
Only to see it melt by day before the onslaught of the
Sun's rays; thus does my fickle lover disport himself!

Could I but prepare tea with viper's venom till it turned
Yellow, then to my lover untrue serve so potent a brew!

As for he who causes strife between my lover and me, may the
Lord shrivel the blossom on his tree and dry up his fountains!

Be not wrathful in your aching heart, women are
Naught but treachery and deceit incarnate!

'Twas covetousness that brought the fish out of the water;
Else, being a fine swimmer, he would have avoided capture!

Tell me this: ask the stone which hath rolled to the foot of the
hill
Whether it is ready to face the upward slope once more?

Now you have a foal purchased, go try him with a
Saddle; see how he fares on the slope!

Who then will to my lover send word? I am encamped upon
The forested peak, have naught but tea to drink!

My love for you is like unto that of the hunter who recalls the
joys of
The chase; he scales the wooded heights to corner thee, O wild
beast!

I have consorted with many a red-cheeked maid, yet, I do declare,
There's none so fair as can compare with mounting a swift charger!

Love is like unto a punishing ride on horseback;
I am so saddle-sore it bids fair to break my bones!

Bear witness, O hills and saints, of what has befallen me!
Since incurable disease was by God inflicted, sleep now
Forsakes me. For bullet-wound a cure would find,

Would weep for a departed kinsman, solace to find;
Grievous slight have I at my sweetheart's hands suffer'd!

'Tis in my mother's tongue,
O beloved, that my passion I do declare.
But how will fare those who, of a day,
To speak Tamazight do not dare?
Words of love will ne'er say!

O gallant cavalier, O frequenter of the highways and by-ways,
Feed your white steed fodder aplenty, but spare not your spurs,
The vengeful ones have sworn to cut off your head!

O jackal, in the plain the herdsman will ambush you,
Climb yon mountain, the stock-breeder lies in wait!

The heart of him rejoices who has wed a comely bride,
But as to the man whose wife is ugly, he be like the homeward
Bound muleteer, who has naught purchased nor his debts paid!

O the taste of well-sugared mint tea; O for the lips of young girls;
O for lusty, full-breasted women; were it not for the expense!

In water did I bathe, but my friend's perfume ne'er did leave me;
It hath penetrated the very marrow of my bones!

Could I but know: does he use soap in paradise?
Does candle-light still brighten his nightly vigil?
Has his countenance changed since last we met?

Should I resume my travels, I will e'er curse you, O cemetery,
For stealing my lover, leaving me here alone and forlorn!

On setting off down the track, I looked back and beheld
My lover's castle; full many a bitter tear did I shed!

Take with you on your travels this curl as a love-token,
Lest temptation treacherous entice you down trails untrodden!

O cleric, I suffer neither from headache nor road-weariness.
Love-sickness alone causes me this grievous suffering!

'Tis well-known that hair does link head to heart,
Love-sickness has made my hair turn snow-white!

The preacher's a liar, paradise and women are of one
Kin; the appreciation of beauty ne'er was a sin!

'Tell me, O cleric, surely there's no harm if my
Darling stays at home during the month of fasting.'
'Fickle be beauty', answered he, 'Beware of
Your woman; to kiss her lips is sinful!'

Honey is on my lover's lip; 'tis a fact,
Bees ne'er gather pollen from palm-leaves!

A glance at the centre of the encampment I did cast –
Not a soul in sight; has departed my heart's delight!

When shines the moon and all good Muslims slumber,
This poet alone and running water shun restfulness.

Put your trust in me if you are confident;
When you see acorns on juniper trees,
When you see cats with mice consorting,
When you see camels with iron-shod hooves,
Then shall be the day of our parting!

Whence came this hoary head and beard most grey?
From the twists and travails of unhappy love affairs!

Could I but experience once more my period of glory!
Could I but change my bones for those of a youngster.
Insultingly did Fadma say: 'See how white is your beard!'

Attempt not, O stomach, to inflate yourself,
Attempt not my countenance to change;
Fated to die am I, 'tis in the sky written!

Dust to dust, man 'neath earth returns,
For each birth 'tis another life that goes;
Fated to die am I, 'tis written in the sky!

Life is not unlike a decaying carcass, yet
God gave it the semblance of a grazing gazelle.
Across the plain she lures the unheeding hunter,
Death claims him as he is about to catch her!

Typical short snatches of verse, timeless in origin, of the *tamawayt*
genre. Some were collected by me from Fatima Elasri, Haj Qeddur
(Ayt Myill), in the spring of 1993; others are culled from different
sources, mostly *Isaffen Ghbanin* (1993).

The context for these verses is that of the Berbers in their Heroic
Age, a feuding society where honour is all, where young maidens
are as beautiful as they are dutiful when married, while men, many
of them affected by wander-lust in keeping with their nomadic
habits, are handsome and bold, ready to defend their honour knife
in hand. Such verse is characterised by choice euphemism and
symbolism, fraught with local imagery, often intelligible to local
Imazighen alone.

VERSE FROM THE RIF AND BENI ZNASSEN AREAS OF NORTHERN MORROCO

Ode to Sidi Muhand Amezian

Freezing cold blasts of wind blow
In the Rumi's hot-water kettle!
To test the enemy God did send the
Bravest of all Rifian fighters!
Who else but Sidi Muhand in person?!
'Twas he who came against the Rumi!

O Sidi Muhand Amezian,
O bold Holy War fighter!
With his left hand death doth deal,
With his right hand doth likewise.
Thanks to Mauser rifle bright and new
Doth set aflame the field of valour!

In final battle did Sidi Muhand fall,
The happy Rumi, his body in a cart placed.
Alas! Gone the moon, gone the stars!
Sidi Muhand, O bold Holy War fighter!
The rain mourneth thy death, drought
For two years was rife – sad the moon!

Collected by Abdslam Khalafi (2004, 62–4)

This little poem recalls the short-lived fame of Shrif Muhand Amezian who, from 1908 till his death in 1912, led the resistance in the Rif against Spain.

Battle of Dhar Ubarran

Captain Byarepya against Temsamam did march,
Hoping like a defenceless flower to pluck it.
Little knew what an impregnable place it was!
Came the Ayt Waryaghar fighters, young and old,
Boldly faced the foe and unto him, the ogre,
Did what the fishermen with his net doth to fish!
Of the enemy, twelve hundred the Ayt Waryaghar did slay,
Only five returned home the sorry tale to tell!

Collected by Abdslam Khalafi (2004, 63).

A poetic fragment on the battle of Dhar Ubarran (better known as Anwal), where in 1921 General Silvestre with a Spanish army of several thousand soldiers suffered the worst defeat the colonial powers ever endured in Africa.

Monkey business with turtles

Long ago in a far off forest, a colony of monkeys did dwell.
A king they had, Qardin was his name and long did he reign.
When his time came, to designate a successor was necessary.
As was their wont, old monarch and young challenger in a
Contest indulged, to settle the issue of succession.

Together the two did fight, till Qardin was defeated.
His head hanging in shame the forest he did leave.
To the river-bank he retreated, where grew a fig tree,
Amidst whose branches sanctuary did find, and
Sustenance drew from the figs that there grew.

Some of the figs he would throw into the water below,
Where dwelt a turtle, which became grateful for such bounty.
Though Qardin of falling figs the splashing sound enjoyed,
At length he also acquired himself a friend tried and true,
Though in sooth that turtle his mate did neglect.

By her husband's frequent absences aggriev'd, the turtle
Council did take with a neighbour, who advised trickery:
'Dost thou feign sickness, so that thy husband will return.
Then suggest a remedy – a monkey's heart, nothing less!'
Sad the turtle, neither friend nor spouse wishing to lose!

Deciding his mate to keep, the turtle to the tree returned.
'My friend, come to my house apples and bananas to eat!'
The invitation accepted Qardin on his friend's back did jump.
Of two minds whether to his friend the matter to broach,
The turtle swam some distant, then slowed to a stop.

'Wouldst thou do me a favour? See now, my good friend,
For my ailing mate, a monkey's heart is the only cure!'
Should Qardin refuse, would entail death by drowning.
Better by far to play for time. 'See now!' he replied,
'Willing am I to help thee, my heart shall surely have!'

'There be but one obstacle. When a monkey is on
Travel, for safe-keeping at home his heart doth leave.
Return me therefore to my tree, my heart for to fetch!'
The turtle took Qardin to the tree into whose branches he
Leap'd, saying: ' 'Twould indeed be silly to give my heart!'

From a traditional Berber text in Beni Znassen dialect recited by her uncle Dali to Khadija Hraoui, one of my oral literature students at Mohammed V University, Rabat, Spring 1987.

The folklore specialist will no doubt recognize here a Berber version of an episode contained in *Kalila wa-Dimna*, the Arabic fables, itself inspired by the *Fables of Bidpai* from India.

Short poetic fragments

Didst think I was left unscath'd by thy insulting remark?
Verily, was worse than horse's hoof its mark on my heart,
That hammer or pickaxe is powerless to remove!

Mother dear, what of this affliction that killeth me?
This day, lizards are more venomous than vipers,
This day, like brave men vile cowards aspire to glory!

In the market a Jew I did find haggling over the price of a rifle;
Methinks hath acquired martial ambition, hath designs upon us!

O Muha, O my Muh! Please, on my behalf to Tangier
Must thou go, now that waves are calm; lies like a mill-pond
The sea. Pray bring me cartridges for Mauser rifle to fit!

Nightly doth the lion roar along the Melwiya banks!
The sound hath carried far into the hills, far into Trifa
country! Better death than humiliation!

O Mistress Melwiya of the blue pebbles!
Of Mama take good care when she crosseth thy waters;
Send no cold wind, make light her way!

Verse from the Rif and Beni Znassen areas of Northern Morroco

Let no one frequent thee, O mountain of Azru Hammar,
Since young Mama was there seen in a Rumi's company!

From dawn to dusk did patiently observe the pass,
Vainly waiting for Mama's messenger, who cameth not!

Couplets and tercets called *izran* in Rif and Beni Znassen oral
tradition, collected by A. Renisio (1932).

Some of the themes here – pride, concern for Muslim woman-
hood, references to Jews – are characteristic of Berber love poetry
irrespective of region, while others reflect the atmosphere of the
early 1920s and the changes sparked by colonial conquest.

POETRY FROM MOROCCO'S SOUTH-WEST

Legend of Tamdult Waqqa

With folk from Tamdult Waqqa few can compare,
Yet such was their pride it did encompass their fall!
Of the Sektana, pray tell me, what are their origins?
A Sektani pure and true can but hail from Tamdult!
But what of Tamdult Waqqa, what of its history!
In that city did live a man with no male progeny.
Had but fair daughters four, hale and hearty,
In a garden outside the city he cultivated fruit,
Where his daughters daily his repast did bring.
Evil-doers were wont to molest them, stealing
And eating provisions for their father destined.
Once, twice, thrice were the girls thus waylaid.
On the fourth occasion 'neath some cow-dung
Was placed their sire's repast!

Upon finding this the evil-doers let them go.
To them their father did say: 'Tell me, pray,
Wherefore bringest me cow-dung this day?'
Answered the girls: 'He who cannot on
Siblings' protection rely, to eat dung is fated!'
Tearfully their sire made reply: 'Tell me,
Daughters dear, what hath come to pass?'
'Three times did we your repast bring,
Three times was it by robbers stolen!'

Whereupon he swore: 'Daughters dear,
One fated day, reparation shall ye obtain!'

He went and made appropriate sacrifice to a chief
Named Muhammad Ali Amensag, who answered:
'Return to thy home and when such a month shall
Come to pass, by night shall we invade thy city!
Do thou put a mark on thy house, verily shall
The *harka* scathless leave thy property!'
The man counted the days till came to pass the
Month appointed, then on his house a mark did put.

The people of Tamdult Waqqa had a divineress,
'A *harka* is heading this way!' quoth she,
'The cavaliers' horse-shoes are mounted back to front!'
''Tis but falsehood!' replied the unbelieving citizens.
Down on them the *harka* came, wrought destruction
Great, and far and wide dispers'd the inhabitants.
He who hails from Tamdult has a genuine pedigree,
He who from there hails not is an impostor, a *burtgiz*!

As for us, our forefathers from Tamdult did come.
'Tis our origin, we whose abode is at Tinfat.
Forsooth, our men-folk of *barud* are not afeard!
When we of Tinfat a-soldiering go, enemies
Tremble, they who surround us, even though
Our ranks number barely four hundred marksmen.
The four thousand marksmen of our Sektana rivals
Have we decisively vanquished in battle royal,
Till came a day when the Zenaga and their *harkas*
Came against us with their fifty-eight tribes!
They surrounded us, dug trenches and till
Exhaustion battled on. Took Tirzi, also Gunin;

In Ifran were we confined and beleaguered!
Of our marksmen a hundred and thirty they slew,
No quarter asked nor given, to each his due!
Of the Ayt Ighri were the chieftains slain, nor were
Those of Ayt Abd al-Wirt and Imadidn spared!
Yet to Marrakesh our Sektana enemies did go,
Brought in their train El Haj Thami al-Glawi!

This is an ancient *qaçida*, by an unknown Sektani poet
from Tinfat, collected by Colonel Justinard and contained
in his *Le Tazeroualt*.

In some ways this is the foundation myth of the Sous Berbers, as
many a tribe down there has links to Tamdult, imagined or real. The
poem is possibly based on an eleventh-century episode of the
Almoravid conquest, when the religious zealots sacked this Khariji
stronghold, although it probably waxed and waned afresh before its
final ruin. The poem casts a casual glance at south-west Morocco's
cruel medieval past, fraught with alarums and excursions, when the
smell of gun-powder (*barud*) frequently tainted the air as some clan
launched a military expedition (*harka*) on its rival. Compared to
many such pieces it is interesting that at no point do we find the
slightest reference to God. The poem centres on Tinfat, whose
warlike inhabitants claim descent from those of Tamdult, originally
expelled from their ancestral home. For a city with a tarnished
reputation like Sodom and Gomorrah, one is struck by the mildness
of its shortcomings. It would appear that the relatively minor slight
to a man's honour barely justifies the destruction of a whole city.
But then honour was all in the social framework of those troubled
times. The over-simplified figures, four hundred heroes against four
thousand enemies gives the poem an epic, timeless note, while the
allusion to *burtgiz*, reminds us that the Portuguese were active in
the Souss in the sixteenth and seventeenth centuries. Finally, a

closing reference to al-Glawi, the famous pasha of Marrakesh who
played golf with Winston Churchill, well-known to British readers
through the endeavours of Gavin Maxwell (1966), brings one right
up to the twentieth century!

The story of Sheddad Ibn Aad

In God's name, this my tale shall tell
Of this world, its beauty and misery!
Have mercy on us, the end of time is at hand!
Of moderation may thy spirit have its share.
If lust tempts thee, may destroy thee,
Stones strike us, break our arms and legs,
E'en in death doth the grave consume us!
He whose passion the orange craveth
Must his orange-grove plant, then cherish it,
With nary a care, though life is not everlasting!
Where is God's emissary, Al-Buraq the horseman?
What of Hassan's children – to dust reduced?!
And Lahssen and Lhusseyn – pigeons in Paradise!
Time, run thy course; where art thou, O yesterday?
By today replaced. Without thee no eternity, O God!

Now what of Sheddad who had a rampart built,
Finely gold-decorated with foundations of iron,
Had built an Eighth Paradise, and did sit there.
Sacred psalms did sing and worshipped God,
Who abideth aloft in the Seventh Heaven.
Stealthily came Satan: 'Why worship the
Master of the Skies? Verily the paradise
That thou seekest is here, close at hand!'

Sheddad follow'd in Satan's path, pray'd no more.
One day came the Angel of Death, to him did say:
'Verily, thy peace must make with thy Maker!'
Sheddad did reply: ' 'Fore God, give me a week,
That I take leave of them that incarnate beauty!'

Sheddad in his little Heaven sought refuge,
Closed the doors; came the Angel of Death,
To him did say: 'Come, 'tis time we went!'
'In God's name! Grant me but a day, or two!'
'Agreed! A final reprieve I grant thee, till tomorrow!'
Satan to him appear'd and said: 'Mount thy black
Steed and gallop away, out from Here Below!'
Far and away he rode till the brave beast founder'd.
Satan follow'd him up, said: 'Enter thy horse!'
Thus in his horse's belly did Sheddad find refuge.
The Angel of Death arriv'd hotfoot and said:
'Time hath run out, sirrah! Hast nowhere to hide!'
Sheddad's soul away was borne his body unbath'd,
Received neither winding-sheet, nor grave;
Is to Hell's fires everlastingly condemned!

A traditional, pedagogical ballad of the *qaçida* genre by an
unknown author, based on a well-known, pre-Islamic legend, of
which there are many versions; first published by Justinard.

This poem deals with the theme of time, linked to the inevitability
of death. Each one on this earth may live but the time allotted to
him – an inescapable truism. Interestingly, the poem contains an
allusion to *tawakhir n-zzman* ('the end of time'), an ill-defined
notion already seen in some Middle Atlas poems.

Ode to Yamina Mansur

O Yamina Mansur, may the Almighty prolong thy days,
Make thee great-hearted, thy beauty everlasting!
Proud *qayd* Tayb, 'tis a fact, to thy sire did letters send,
Saying: 'Grant me thy daughter's hand; 'twill be a good
Match. In exchange Azanif and Tinzert shall be yours!'
Thus spake Sheikh Mansur to his daughter: 'Pray listen,
Yamina, for husband the Pasha shalt thou take, he the
Sultan's representative, blessed by Angels on high!'
Quoth Yamina to her father: 'Put aside such words,
Father dear, were the whole High Atlas with gold pav'd
I would not, for one second, contemplate such a match!'

Thus spake Sheikh Mansur to his daughter: 'Pray listen,
Yamina, e'en though his suit thou dost refuse,
Outside the law *qayd* Ludini will not hesitate to act!'
Quoth Yamina to her father: 'Put aside such words,
Father dear, in the assembly, that association of power
And enmity, how will other leaders thy council heed?'
Thus spake Sheikh Mansur to his daughter: 'Pray listen,
Yamina, thou may ignore Ludini, yet into his hands
The law will take!' Quoth Yamina to her father:
'Put aside such words, Father dear, upon my head,
Henna and silken scarves I do swear, ne'er shall it
Be by enemy said: "A slave hath Yamina wed!" '

To the Seventh Heaven shall repair the Mansur family,
There to build fortress stout, far from this our river.
Up there shall be our existence, O father, on the mountain,
Far from Ludini and his minions, till death him doth claim!'
Thus spake the sheikh to his daughter: 'So be it, Yamina!'

Then did Ludini his army of locusts muster, and at its
Head laid waste Aqeshtim's village and fields!
With his family towards the heights Mansur retreated!
Consider the Ayt Aqeshtim – such valorous warriors, are
Folk of the silken belts who, to a man, ever keep their word!
Let misfortune be Ludini's lot, let him burn in hell!
For uttering words untoward, O Lord, thy pardon I do implore!
O Yamina Mansur, may the Almighty prolong thy days,
Make thee great-hearted, thy beauty everlasting!

A traditional nineteenth-century ballad of the *qaçida* genre, attributed
to the poet Lhaj Ahmad ben Abdellah and collected by Colonel
Justinard (cf. *Revue du Monde Musulman*, vol. LX, pp. 94–5, 1925).

The poem tells the story of the high-minded daughter of a sheikh of
the Aqeshtim clan (Induzal tribe), living on the north slopes of the
Anti-Atlas, and of her refusal to marry local bigwig, *qayd* Tayb
Ludini, then governor of Tarudannt, probably under Sultan Mulay
Sliman. Though such a refusal is tantamount to the Aqeshtim
clan's self-destruction, in a land where might is right, Yamina
remains unflinching in her resolve that, in exchange for two
villages, she will not be married off to an *ismegh* ('slave', or 'dark-
skinned individual'), for Ludini, so we are told, was a Bwakher
from Meknes, a descendant of Mulay Ismail's guard originally
brought into Morocco from the Sudan – a trait that smacks of
underlying racial discrimination. Note the father's delicacy, in that
he refrains from forcing his daughter into a marriage that may be
distasteful to her.

Ayt Ba Amran verbal joust

Off I went to Gwelmim, there to find tea and amber;
At Ksabi met with beauty, but precious little pleasure!
Towards Anja made my way but fell in with foot-pads.
'O wealthy Shelluh traveller, stand and deliver!'
The Sbuia to eat have honey, 'tis ever ready,
But of meat and vegetable stew have none to offer.
As for the Ayt Khoms, they have Sheikh Seyd,
The Akhsas tribe are renowned caravaneers!

Thus spake Yahya Umghar to Ayt Khoms women:
'Do ye make of silk and henna your business,
Shall concern myself with flint and gun-powder to
Prevent the enemy from penetrating our homeland!'
Yahya Umghar's steed is as swift as the wind,
Attempt not, O muleteer, to keep up with him!

Your grain, Uld Awragh, from Wad Nun to Tafilalt
Did go; whence camels to the Orient convey'd it!

'Tis a fact, proud-hearted falcons are the Imestitn,
Oxen never sacrifice, nor do they ask for quarter,
They know but God and the keen-edged blade!

Thus spake the girls of Tangarfa to those of Taliwin:
'Perfume, myrtle and carnation do we renounce, so
Long as shaggy-headed Azwafid men are amongst us!'

When thou divided the Ayt Ba Amran tribe, O war,
The fighting clans assembled at Lmers, others at Tangarfa,
On Khmis market-place was yet another muster!

O Ayt Ba Amran, do ye sell your bushels of wheat,

Barter them for flint, lead, and gun-powder!
Let us rouse the Igzuln, for they are like dead men,
Departed their doughty warriors, gone one after t'other.
May the Lord strengthen thy sword-arm, O Yahya Umghar!
And thee too, O Bu Hiya; also Kamal from Azilal,
And proud Ayssa n-Umbark from the Asserir lands!

These are excerpts from a verbal joust, probably of nineteenth-century vintage, between two famous Shelluh poets Aomar u-Sherra of Ayt Yub (Ayt Khoms alliance), and Uld Awragh of the Imestitn (Sbuyia alliance). It was collected by Colonel Justinard.

The lines illuminate a time of widespread intra-tribal warfare. After a Sbuyia alliance victory the Azwafid clan had occupied Tangarfa, hence the local women's lament. Yahya Umghar, a warrior famous for his bravery, was grandfather to Sheikh Seyd.

Pedagogical poem (I)

Dispers'd our friends – some thou have claim'd, O grave!
Others, deviating from the path, to Satan now belong!
It behoveth me little, if for a week we can eat flowers;
Heaven, thou canst be as nothing to Earth,
O horse! Such beauty, such grace – effortless thy gallop!
Yet for one small reason, all people do forsake thee,
'Coz of a thousand spur-thrusts against thy saddle-carpet!
'Tis of prayer the rampart! In God's name, whomsoever
Recognizeth it, shall with the Almighty find favour!

With forc'd friendship, my friend, will have no truck!
Is but meaningful if one heart truly loveth another!
Most folk today in the desert will abandon thee,

And, pray, from whence shall come thy help?!
'Fore God, he who slayeth thee, thy corpse
Shall leave on the ground, unwash'd, unburied!
O unworthy sons of Adam, ye are like the rock on
Which water falleth, yet no grass nor flower groweth!

Like unto a motherless orphan is our country, having
Just lost its father – such was Mulay al-Hassan!
O earthly life, to be accomplish'd, dead must be thy heart,
For aspirations, e'en a monarch to fulfil them is powerless!
Quoth the lion to the panther: 'Peace upon thee!
Let us between us the forest share, be its sole owners!'
Alas! Methinks the falcon I did espy, yet not having
Clearly seen its distinctive marks, on it cannot swear!
May the Lord be with you, O son well-born!
'Coz his master he doth constantly praise.
Didst e'er see a falcon on earth replanting seeds?
Nay, 'tis on high that he buildeth his eyrie!

A traditional pedagogical poem from Ayt Ba Amran, a tribal area
close to Sidi Ifni in south-west Morocco, also collected by Justinard.

The notion of eating flowers evokes a time of plenty. Otherwise a
jumble of ideas: about the horseman who, by spurring on his steed,
insults the prayer-carpet beneath his saddle; the usual truism about
mankind being generally iniquitous; regret at the passing of Mulay
Hassan I (which situates this poem in the mid-1890s); a conclusion
containing four different, short parables reflecting on everyday life.

Pedagogical poem (II)

Even if camel caravans from Gharb salt should bring,
None shall have beauty unless God hath ordain'd it!
For heifers butter-milk, with songs goeth good cheer.
To the foot of the cliff did the falcon the partridge chase.
But my desire pursueth the possessor of beauty,
Nor shall I ever forget the place where she resideth!
Curse the demon, that wicked enemy of thine,
Curse the deceitful one who trieth to outshine him!
Better to show a bold front than seek refuge in flight;
Better to be vanquish'd than live with regrets eternal,
Better death than expecting mercy from one's enemy!
Better to eat wild melons, than succumb to hunger!

During the ploughing season 'twas ill-advis'd to rest.
When reaping barley, of scant harvest I did complain.
If a-hunting we should go, safer to keep one's eyes open,
Lest from the hunter we should become the hunted!

From peak to peak doth the mouflon leap in his quest for
Water. To shoot him the huntsman must e'er keep ahead.
O gazelles, this mountain can no longer your sanctuary be,
As soon as he can shoot, thither goeth man for sport!
A saddle can take but one cavalier, no place for two!
The eye containeth but water, 'tis not fit for a thorn!
In thy plate shalt find but what thou art fated to eat!

Remain e'er active on thy feet, shalt derive profit thereon,
Another man his feet will keep for kicking mother's son!
Hark the loud-mouth's prattle, much hath befallen him!
The man who seeth me with my copper-sheath'd scabbard,
Little knoweth of the death-dealing blade it doth contain!

Did I not say: 'A reed maketh for fire a poor bed-fellow!
Persian china-ware is fine to look at but hath little use!'
A suitable perch did the falcon vainly seek;
Finally, in a thorn-tree did alight: 'twas of no avail!

A palm-tree hath an olive produc'd! Tell me, brother,
Why did it not yield a date? Each man his monarch doth
Proclaim. The *ayt bariz* are my sovereigns, that is plain!
Digging a deep hole in the ground, for Evil I did find a final
Resting-place. Cannot forgive the fool who along did come
With pick and spade, sought to disinter it!

Salt to speech giveth flavour, flour staveth off hunger,
Whichever way one goeth about it, in a dispute
'Taint with hands, but sharp words that hurt is inflicted!
Thanks to thine eyes, thy head shalt not hit thy porch!
A poverty-stricken farmer, to plough his furrow is oblig'd,
Should he from an ailment suffer, let him go to the *agurram*.

This traditional pedagogical piece was included in Justinard's
collection of poems from Ayt Ba Amran.

The poem consists of a string of semi-truisms and proverb-like
utterances aimed at enriching the audience's knowledge of worldly
matters. The time-serving reference to the predominance of the *ayt
bariz*, or 'the folk from Paris' (i.e. the French), plainly situates this
poem in the second decade of the twentieth century, by which time
Berbers from the area were making their way to France to find work
by hook or by crook.

Ode to Sidi Hmad u-Musa

O Sidi Hmad u-Musa, a visit to your tomb is like
That of a pilgrimage to Mecca without fatigue!
O living saints, and ye, O illustrious dead,
I do beseech ye: may my source ne'er run dry,
My industrious millstone for to grind!
O Sidi Hmad u-Musa, whene'er I call on thee,
Through thick and thin be thou my defender!
Like falcon's eyrie on mountain-steep,
Be my succour when, with wind-blown sail,
My ship steereth through shark-fill'd waters!
He who hopeth that God his wishes may fulfil,
Shall, every month, to saints' tomb repair,
Nor forget on Friday alms for the mosque!
Sidna Malek, didst thou not say: 'When a
Man hunteth, to God and saints doth pray
That they may gazelle or wild sheep send!
Not a jackal whose stench is borne on the wind!'

The author of this poem is unknown, but it was collected
by Ahmed Benzekri, in spring 1988, in connection with
my oral literature workshop at the Faculty of Letters,
Rabat. The first two lines are from A. Lakhsassi's article
'Ziyara to the tomb of Sidi Hmad u-Musa'.

This short poem is addressed to Sidi Hmad u-Musa, the leading
agurram of the Sous area, whose tomb in the Tazerwalt mountains
south-east of Tiznit is visited by pilgrims at a great yearly festival,
and plays the role of a poor man's *hajj*.

A letter am I sending

A letter am I sending, God speed it on its way!
Beloved be the folk known to me in Essawira!
Passionate longing for her is killing me,
I see her no more, she has vanished;
Go there I could if I so wished.
But methinks I might not find you;
Sore would be my feet, wasted my time!
A letter am I sending, God speed it on its way!

Anxiety and worry have torn at my heart,
What is to be done? Am still on roads lost!
Who shall hear my complaints, or believe me?
May God help me, from my mind banish her!
Nor e'er again be in love's toils enmeshed!
True man must always reasonable be
And with sensible folk consort!
A letter am I sending, God speed it on its way!

O head of mine, sense have you sadly lacked!
What need have you of such an unworthy lover,
Who cares little for you, and yet we forgive her!
If she comes searching we shall avoid her!
O lover, had your intentions been pure,
Ne'er would idle gossip have separated us!
A letter am I sending, God speed it on its way!

I forgive you, knowing you for what you are!
In my deepest heart and thoughts did hold you
Dear, thinking true love to have found!
Never did dream that you would deceive me!
Forsooth, now I know you for what you are!

Neither love nor passion for me do feel!
A letter am I sending, God speed it on its way!

Verily has my time with you been wasted,
Since we share nothing, in word or deed,
Thoughtlessly did I act – so much I admit!
When I trusted you in my heart of hearts,
And did to the skies glorify and praise you,
Scant gratitude did show for my goodness!
A letter am I sending, God speed it on its way!

What need have I of your love and company?
Whoever desires you may your lover become!
As for me, I do swear – mark my word –
Nevermore will I to your charms succumb!

Whoever yearns for you may your lover be,
Nor should think that I am to distraction driven,
You interest me not, plain to see is your vanity!
A letter am I sending, God speed it on its way!

Look you, men who accept with you to consort,
Are those who truthfully know aught about you!
True, men of pride and dignity will accept not to
Frequent you, nor shall they importance grant you!
A letter am I sending, God speed it on its way!

This is a contemporary *amarg*-style poem, as sung by the
famous *rayss* Akhattab, was collected in the autumn of
1986 by Khadija Battu, a member of my Oral Literature
Workshop at the Faculty of Letters, Mohammed V
University, Rabat. Khadija's parents originally came from
the Ayt Wadjass tribe, near Ssuq al-Had Imulas in the High
Atlas foothills north of Tarudannt.

The poet mourns his lost love living in the seaside town of Essawira, known as Tassurt, in Berber. An historically important place, it is situated at the north-west corner of the Tashelhit-speaking area, home to the Haha tribe.

Fadma

Oh that my heart were a chamber to be unlocked,
Then would see, my beloved, how it burns for you!
Have grown accustomed to your lips – what's to be done?
When I forget your name heaven and earth start weeping!
O Fadma, you are like choice honey in a marble bowl,
From which may partake none but the mightiest kings!
O Fadma, for you does the deft-fingered craftsman
Carefully work gold, your shapely neck to fit!
O Fadma, you are a queen, as yet uncrowned,
Yet to her have all tribes sworn allegiance!
O Fadma, which *agurram* did your parents visit?
When you saw light of day, Heaven and Earth rejoiced!

A traditional *amarg*-style love poem, whose original author is unknown. It comes from the Sous region and was collected by Ahmed Benzekri, one of my oral literature students, in Spring 1988.

Fadl and Aytush

Once upon a time and long ago lived beautiful
Aytush whom handsome Fadl did dearly love!
Love so strong they vowed ne'er to be separated,

Night and day spending in each others' company!
One day the king the lovers did descry and to his
Servant spoke: 'Let them in my palace sleep tonight!'
They accepted, but to separate places were shown.
Came morning and after his love Fadl did inquire.
'Nay, go thou may, but Aytush here shall stay!'

In total disarray, upon his horse Fadl rode away.
The king took Aytush for wife and behind fourteen
Doors, for his bride a luxurious abode did provide.
For her solace, two gazelles he had made, one
Of gold, one of silver; but, do as he might, never
Could she the vows forget 'twixt her and her lover!
From her vantage-point up a tall tower, Aytush did
Espy Fadl on horseback, indulging in powder-play.
The king, she knew, would from dawn to midday
Tarry, was ne'er by her side in the afternoon.

To fetch her lover a servant she did despatch, who said:
'Sidi Fadl! From my mistress greetings, what sayest thou?'
'O peerless servant, how can I the royal palace enter?'
'Fasten thy sandals. Put a veil over any door thou reachest,
Then forget not to close it. Have faith, all shall be well!'
Carefully, by the servant escorted, he gained admittance,
Long night of love did spend with his beloved Aytush,
Left at dawn, but – fatal error – his perfume box forgot!
Returning, the king the offending box did find, then knew,
For sure, some base interloper had played him false!

To cover his tracks, Fadl forthwith to the blacksmith did
Repair, bade him make new box, the old one to replace!
The king summoned his courtiers, of their perfume boxes
Ordered the inspection. Each man did say: 'Nay, Majesty,

'Tis but my old used one!' All, that is, except for Fadl!
At which the king waxed wroth, shouting: 'The miscreant
Hath himself betrayed. O courtiers, strike down this Jew!'
From her tower Aytush can see what has come to pass,
To her lover calls out: 'In God must thou trust, O Fadl,
Remember, love and sacrifice shall ever companions be!'

Fadl with his maker made peace; then was there no
Staying blow most fatal; in the dust Fadl's head did roll.
Whereupon, from her tower, Aytush took a running
Jump, but to dust was turned ere the ground she struck!
At the northern end of the grave-yard, was one lover interred,
T'other at the southern end. Yet at dawn two palm-trees did
Grow, their branches intertwined! Angrily the king bade his
Men cut them down – to no avail! Along came a Jew, who said:
'What shalt thou give me, if to thy problem solution can find?'
'Name thy price, but, pray, of these trees rid my sight!'
A quintal of wax was all it took the trees to commit to flames;
Ne'er grew again! The Jew his reward pocketed, but early next
Morning did fountains two gush from the lovers' tombs!

This poem is a reconstruction of a mixed prose and verse version
collected for me from her mother by Fatima Ahloullay (Ayt Swab, Tiznit
region) in the winter of 1985–6, and another version in rhythmic prose
(Agrour, 2007, 29–9).

This is *the* basic Moroccan love story, known elsewhere in Arabic-
speaking areas as *Kan ya ma kan* ('Once upon a time'), as 'Sbou and
Melwiya' in the Middle Atlas, and certainly widespread in the Sous.
The hopeless love theme and tragic ending are strongly reminiscent
of a Celtic tale, 'Deirdre and the sons of Uisneach'.

Hemmu u-Namir

Far from his parents, Hemmu u-Namir pined after love.
Hemmu was a vivacious, pleasure-loving youth who
Would sleep the night away till dawn and then arise.
Mysteriously gilded with henna his hands did find.
Beaten by his catechist he never complained, though
On him rained down harsh words and blows!
He pressed the boy to say why his hands were painted.
Tearfully did the boy echo: 'Sir, I sleep till dawn!
Henna on my hand I do discover without seeing a soul,
What shall I do if invisible beings with me consort?
I doze till early morning then see someone with
The semblance of an angel henna to my hands applying!'

'Deceitful Hemmu, this is naught but play-acting!'
Then for a week closely did the catechist watch Hemmu!
To Hemmu she did appear like the sun in the gloaming,
'God has sent you here!' said Hemmu, greatly rejoicing:
To my humble abode be welcome, my dear!
For sweet fiery beauty like yours 'tis hardship too severe,
Such a heavy heart I endure – cannot cure my malady!'
Interrupting him, the apparition did reply:
'Pray hold out your hand that I may henna apply
Ere I go, yet surely my pledge you shall ne'er fulfil.'
'Whatever your conditions, accomplish them I will.
If you request hunted animals, gazelles I shall slay,
Should you gold demand, the floor I will cover!'

'Farewell', she replied, 'No wealth, no gold, nor jewels
Do I ask for – but to my request your pledged word!'
Hemmu swore that her conditions he would respect.
Said she: 'A house where no one shall I see but you;

Fourteen chambers one on top of t'other, only one key,
Where, except for God and you, none shall see me!
Your father and mother shall I never see, nor they me!
For meals, ask your mother to prepare portions two.'
Seven stately undetached domes did Hemmu erect,
The key he gave her, in his bosom the secret kept,
Silk-adorned and elated he rendered her!

On a day of days, with his friends a-hunting he did go.
With God and saints he pleaded upon him to bestow
A gazelle, in her eyes for to win great favour.
Hemmu's mother of these things received intelligence,
From Satan, who to her did say: 'That's your reward!
Hemmu correctly learned the desired revelation,
Goes to school no more and recently his nuptials
Did celebrate with a girl of unrivalled beauty!'
She seized a hatchet, under the devil's guidance.

Wrecked the doors and forced entry into the chamber,
Where sat the long-haired beauty, to inquire about her.
She found her like a bright moon in the heavens shining,
With Earth like diamond upon a hyacinth!
With idle talk did the mother importune her.
'Happy am I and happy is my son!
What is your origin? Who are your folk? Who are
Your brothers and how came you here!'
Tears mingled with words, the angel answered:
'Unhappy are you and unhappy is your son!
For God's sake refraining from prattling!
The hunter did the mouflon chase to mountain peak,
The falcon pursued the partridge – only to lose it!
To your home did destiny's path lead me.
Now leave I must and, aye, pay for trespassing!'

These were the sad tidings that Hemmu received,
The doors he found totally ruined, as he sat there,
In the ground his tears made runnels.
Then his lament to God thus began:
'O God, what have I done? What has come to pass?
Ne'er did I quarrel, nor antagonize a soul, O Lord!
Ne'er did I quarrel, nor swindle a soul, O Lord!
What have I done? Why am I doomed? O Lord!'
The first door he opened, dampness he there did find.
Then the second, the third, the fourth and so on,
Water above his ankles, caused by woman's tears!

Close to death he found her, cadaverous and wan,
In less than a day had her beauty almost gone!
Upon the window-sill perched, thus she spoke:
'Adieu Namir, of your betrayal we have taken note,
Indeed, have my worst fears been confirmed!
Now in God's name I bid you farewell!'
Feathers sprouting by God's will, a bird she
Became, threw him a ring which he carefully kept.
His eyes saw her soar up to the Seventh Heaven,
To her abode among the Golden Towers!
Again, his sad fate did bemoan, to God did complain.
'O Almighty! I beseech you, would that I had
Never wed angel bride, nor moon, because
Wings I do lack to attain the Seventh Heaven!'

Then Hemmu a *ttalb* did consult as to her whereabouts.
'The Seventh Heaven is far, the key to which is a
Green-feathered eagle, a denizen of the mountain-top!'
For departure Hemmu himself did prepare;
To his father he called, urging him to come,
To his mother he called, urging her to come.

'On my head your blessing, O father dear,
On earth shall I roam till death does claim me!
If God calls you to him, we meet in the Hereafter!'
Came the moment of parting as if on pilgrimage.
In tears did leave his brothers, kissed his mother;
Feeling abandoned, his father cried himself blind!
Hemmu saddled his horse and set off on his way.
In despair o'er the earth he wandered for many a day,
In desert places nights and days the youth did spend,
Barley his only fare, nothing but water to drink; a year
Or two, fifteen years, nay thirty or more he roamed.

To the highest mountain-top God led him at length,
There upon the parched ground stood a fruit-tree.
Lo, how green were its leafy branches!
In a loud voice he called out to it saying:
'Far from water you are, far from me my loved one!'
Then in his language an eagle did give tongue:
'O God's creature, answer me, what happened?
What makes you cry? What be your purpose?'

The miserable wanderer thus answered him:
'O green-feathered eagle, where are the Golden
Towers? O eagle of God, can you not see the
Furnace raging, that consumes the heart in me?
In despair have I spent days, months and years.
Let God perceive my sorrow! My companion
Has departed heavenwards, on earth has left me!
Bitter are oleander and death, 'tis well-known,
Yet even greater hurt do feel down to the bone,
Am by love forsaken, so now do spurn all men!'

Thus did the eagle answer: 'Lament not! The
Remorse that haunts you I can cure. To Seventh

Heaven and Golden Towers shall bear you. Now
Slaughter your horse, to provide for the journey!'
To his faithful horse Namir bade sore farewell,
He kissed its hooves, grieving deeply in his heart.
He slew it, thus provoking an agony of distress,
Portions of meat to feed the eagle he did cut off.
Before flying the eagle did jump into a basin of
Boiling water, then a cold one, feathers to strengthen.
Like a comet the eagle bore him through the skies.
As they reached the Sixth Heaven their food gave out.
Hemmu cut flesh from his arm, gave it to the eagle,
Who declared: 'Did I not taste human flesh, O Hemmu?!'
''Twas done for your sake, O eagle!' he replied.
Begged he: 'Pray let me not fall, ere we arrive,
Ready am I arm and leg to remove, can bear the pain!
Arrive we must, the rest behoves me little!'

In the Seventh Heaven did the eagle deposit Hemmu,
Lovelorn youth like an outcast in an alien universe.
Then a fast flowing spring he did descry – sight to
Gladden the eye – and by its side sat down.
Came the angel's slave, from the spring to draw water.
On the surface his fine face reflected she did see;
She dropped everything and ran away in fear!
After her Namir called, begging her to draw near.
'To your mistress my greetings bear. For our acts
On judgment day shall we to account be held!'
To her mistress the servant brought his greetings.
'O sweet angel, let me good tidings bring!'
'Thank you, faithful servant, rejoices my soul.
Happy is my heart, borne aloft by pure delight,
Like he who suddenly unexpected bounty finds;
Namir to us has come, borne by predatory bird!'

The slave showed her the ring Namir had brought.
As the angel took the ring, the past came back.
Tears gushed like a river, love like death she felt.
In the slave's company to the spring she did repair,
And there her Namir did find, with a thoughtful air.
Happily she uttered words of greeting and love:
'O Namir, thus in the Seventh Heaven you find me!
Longing for you has well-nigh killed me, O Hemmu,
Being without news for so many a year!'
Tears and words intermingled, thus did he reply:
'God I did implore! For you was I chastised by my
Teacher. Did leave my father crying, till by tears blinded,
Found no one while to the ends of the earth I roamed,
Did sacrifice my steed, sky-riding eagle for to feed,
My arm was obliged to cut – see here's the mark!
Now have I attained the furthest reaches of heaven!'

By the arm she took him, as would a mother her child.
Heaven's gates overlooking distant Earth she show'd him.
'O Namir, one condition I have to impose, sure as hell,
Just one peep out of this door, and 'tis between us farewell!'
Then spent he seven blissful months in the Seventh Heaven.
On a day of days, with remembrance of home came longing,
Yet his vow did keep. Came of Aïd sacrifice the day.
The gate open, his mother on far distant Earth did espy.
There she stood broken-hearted, with the sacrificial ram.
'O Lord God on high, with whom shall I celebrate?
Where are you, my son, who will slaughter my sheep?
Gone is Hemmu, his old father by sightless eyes afflicted!'
Hearing those words fit to melt stone, to descend he decided.
So, taking one gigantic, galactic leap, earthwards through
Space Hemmu hurtled, like a disintegrating arrow,
Till by God's will his little fingernail, proved enow
Sheep's throat to sever. 'Twas Hemmu's homecoming!

The present poem represents a reconstruction based on two renderings recorded by members of my Oral Literature Workshop at Mohammed V University, Rabat. The first was a folk-tale, containing residual verse passages, recited to Fatima Ahloullay (Ayt Swab of Tiznit) by her mother in the winter of 1985-1986. The second was a poem collected by Ahmed Benzekri in March 1988. 'Hemmu u-Namir', or 'Hmad u-Namir', is a much circulated piece throughout a long swathe of territory between the Sous and Central High Atlas (where I heard yet another version in spring 1988); cf. also Laoust (1949), Peyron (1989), Bounfour (1993), Stroomer (2002), etc.

This is the major epic of the Sous Berbers, exemplifying the incompatibility between mortal and immortal. The poem is usually recited to grown-up audiences only, since Hemmu, visualized as a lecherous *ahwawi*, is not considered a suitable character for children to learn about.

BIBLIOGRAPHY

Agrour, Rachid, *Léopold Justinard, missionaire de la tachelhit*, 1914–54, Paris: Éditions Bouchene (2007).

Arberry, A. J., *Sufism: an account of the Mystics of Islam*, London: George Allen & Unwin (1969).

Berger, François, *Moha ou Hammou le Zaïani; un royaume berbère contemporain au Maroc (1877-1921)*, Marrakech: Éditions de l'Atlas (1929).

Bounfour, Abellah, *Le Nœud de la Langue: langue, littérature et société au Maghreb*, Aix-en-Provence: Édisud (1993).

Drouin, Jeanine, *Un cycle oral hagiographique dans le Moyen-Atlas marocain*, Paris: Sorbonne (1975).

Hamri, Bassou, *La poésie amazigh de l'Atlas central marocain: approche culturelle et analytique*, Doctoral dissertation, Fez University, Dhar el-Mahraz (2005).

Ibn Khaldoun, *Histoire des Berbères*, (trans. Slane, Baron de), 4 vols., Paris: Geuthner (1999).

Justinard, Léopold, 'Poèmes chleuhs recueillis dans le Sous', *Revue du Monde Musulman*, tome LX, 2ᵉ trim., Paris (1925).

Justinard, Léopold, 'Les Aït Ba Amran', *Tribus berbères*, tome 1, Paris: Champion (1930).

Justinard, Léopold, *Un petit royaume berbère: le Tazeroualt*, Paris: Maisonneuve (1954).

Khalafi, Abdslam, 'Resistance poetry from the Rif', *Amazigh Days at Al Akhawayn University: Paving the Way for Tifinagh* (M. Peyron, ed.), Ifrane: AUI Press (2004, pp. 59–64).

Khettouch, Ahmed, *La mauvaise gestion de la cité perçue par un genre littéraire: cas de timdyazin*, Doctoral dissertation, Fez University, Dhar el-Mahraz (2005).

Laoust, Edmond, *Contes berbères du Maroc*, 2 vols., Paris: Larose (1949).

Le Glay, Maurice, *Récits marocains de la Plaine et des Monts*, Paris: Berger-Levrault (1922).

Loubignac, V., *Étude sur le dialecte berbère des Zaïan et Aït Sgougou*, Paris: Leroux (1924).

Maxwell, Gavin, *The Lords of the Atlas*, London: Hodder & Stoughton (1966).

Peyron, Michael, *Rivières Profondes (Isaffen Ghbanin)*, Casablanca: Wallada (1993).

Peyron, Michael, 'Analyse du poème "Hammou Namir" ', conférence AFEMMAM/ EURAMES, Aix-en-Provence (1996).

Peyron, Michael, *The Amazigh Studies Reader*, Ifrane: AUI Press (2006).

Renisio, A., *Étude sur les dialectes berbères des Beni Iznassen, du Rif et des Senhaja de Sraïr*, Paris: Leroux (1932).

Roux, Arsène & Peyron, Michael, *Poésies berbères de l'époque héroïque: Maroc central (1908-1932)*, Aix-en-Provence: Édisud (2002).

Scott O'Connor, V. C., *A Vision of Morocco*, London: Thornton Butterworth (1929).

Skounti, Ahmed, 'Trois poèmes en Tamazight (Haut Atlas)', *AWAL, Cahier d'Études Berbères*, no. 8 (1991, pp. 163–9).

Stroomer, Harry, *Tashelhiyt Berber Folktales from Tazerwalt (South Morocco)*, Köln: Rüdiger Köppe Verlag (2002).

Tharaud, Jérôme & Jean, *Marrakech ou les Seigneurs de l'Atlas*, Paris: Plon (1929).

ACKNOWLEDGEMENTS

Most of the longer Tamazight poems, and some of the short ones contained in this anthology, come from the Arsène Roux archives in Aix-en-Provence to which Claude Brenier-Estrine kindly granted me access between 1999-2001. The Tazizawt corpus was obtained in the field through the help of my friend and travelling companion Houssa Yakobi of Zawit esh-Sheikh (2005–7). My gratitude to Ayesha Azzawi (Ayt Atta) and Labha Elasri (Ayt Myill), colleagues of mine at Al-Akhawayn University, Ifrane.

The remaining short Tamazight poems are from my personal collection, mostly obtained from Ali w Aomar Kadiri of Tunfit (1984–92, Ayt Yhaya tribal region).

Some of the material from the Tashelhit-speaking area came from the endeavours of students attending my Oral Literature Workshop, Rabat Faculty of Letters (1986–8), especially Fatima Ahloullay, Khadija Battou and Ahmed Benzekri. The remainder of the Tashelhit corpus was originally gleaned by Colonel Léopold Justinard early in the twentieth century. My thanks to his son Pierre Justinard for his encouragement; to Rachid Agrour, Colonel Justinard's biographer and also to Abderrahmane Bouchène, copyright holder of the Justinard published material.

Every effort has been made to trace the holders of copyright and to acknowledge the permission of author and/or publisher. If we have failed or made any incorrect attributions, please tell us and corrections will be made in future editions.

INDEX OF POEM TITLES

INDEX OF FIRST LINES

O Yamina Mansur, may the Almighty prolong thy days 102
Off I went to Gwelmim, there to find tea and amber 104
Oh that my heart were a chamber to be unlocked 112
Once upon a time and long ago lived beautiful 112
Pray to the Prophet who surpasseth me, tho' none 15
Pray to the Prophet! As for the caitiff Christian who 33
See the misfortune hidden in my heart; should it on 83
Thou hast neither father nor mother, yet thou 49
Thou visiteth not gnarl'd tree-trunks, O westerly breeze 23
Thus spake Tawjjaaout hill: 'Had it not been for those Zayan 66
Thus spoke Sidi Lmekki: 'By God's grace, let us feast and rejoice 67
Thy name first I utter, O Lord, good companion of 17
Thy name I do first pronounce, O Prophet! Help me that I 25
Thy name I first pronounce, O Muhammad, grant me among 35
Thy name I invoke, O fertiliser of seed 'neath the earth 69
To fresh matters must I now refer, indeed there's much to say 84
Upon the anvil the blacksmith's hammer ringeth! 12
With folk from Tamdult Waqqa few can compare 97
With thy name I do commence, O Lord! 80
Woman! Tarry a while, leave not; tell us truthful tidings! 11
Wouldst thou witness splendour? Then repair to Lenda 59